U.S. Forward Deployment Policy

U.S. Forward Deployment Policy: An Assessment

by

David M. Riester
Major, USAF

THESIS PRESENTED TO THE FACULTY OF THE
SCHOOL OF ADVANCED AIRPOWER STUDIES,
MAXWELL AIR FORCE BASE, ALABAMA, FOR
COMPLETION OF GRADUATION REQUIREMENTS,
ACADEMIC YEAR 1992-93

MAY 1993

Disclaimer

The views expressed in this publication are those of the author and do not reflect the official policy or position of the School of Advanced Airpower Studies, the Air University, the U.S. Air Force or the Department of Defense.

Contents

Abstract

Today, Americans stationed overseas support a defense structure in the North Atlantic Treaty Organization (NATO), Japan, and South Korea built upon past threats. This study hopefully begins a re-evaluation of this forward deployment policy by looking at the history and origins of American participation in the North Atlantic Treaty Organization (NATO). It then compares the original need for forward deployment with today's associated threats, problems and costs.

This study finds that while the United States remains a global power with global interests, forward deployed troops may no longer provide a cost effective means for guarding these worldwide interests. The world threat today may not require a large permanent American presence given the advent of strategic satellite warning, stealth technology, American power projection capabilities, and allied capabilities to defend themselves.

About the Author

Major David M. Riester received a Reserve Officers Training Corps commission from the University of Connecticut in 1978. Following Strategic Air Command tours as a missile combat crew commander and command post controller, and Space Command tours as space orbital analyst, headquarters staff officer, chief of space operations and chief of satellite training, he became the Space and Missile Advisor to the Assistant Secretary of State for Politico-military Affairs, Department of State, Washington D.C. There he implemented the White House's Missile Technology Control Regime, chaired the review of U.S. export licenses relating to the building of foreign space and missile systems, negotiated technology transfer agreements with foreign countries, made weapons proliferation policy, and participated in the political operations during such events as Tiannemen Square, Panama, the evacuation of Somalia, and Operations Desert Shield and Desert Storm. Lieutenant Colonel (select) Riester is a senior missileer with over 400 operational combat crew alerts and wears the master space badge. He received a bachelor's degree in Mathematics from the University of Connecticut and a master's degree in Business Administration from the University of Wyoming. Beginning in June 1993, he will be assigned to J3 operations in Unified Space Command Headquarters, Colorado Springs, Colorado.

I. Introduction

The destruction of the Berlin Wall signified the end of the Cold War and the need to reexamine the costs and benefits of the U.S. forward deployment policy. The forty-five year clash between superpowers required that America maintain 500,000 troops and 400 bases overseas at a cost of 90 billion dollars a year (see Table 1). Containment demanded that 90 percent of the overseas deployed forces reside in Europe, Japan, and South Korea. However, the reduction of superpower competition means that this form of expensive force basing may no longer provide a cost effective means for guarding our worldwide interests.

The world threat today may not require a large permanent American presence given our ability to deploy force rapidly against diminished threats. Strategic warning, stealth technology and American power projection capabilities, as well as allied ability to defend themselves, require that the entire policy of forward deployed forces be re-examined (see Table 1). A serious reappraisal of the U.S. forward deployment policy begins with an examination of the original purpose of the North Atlantic Treaty Organization (NATO), the most successful multilateral security arrangement. The important questions that require an answer are: what do we get for our money and what are the alternatives to the present system?

AMERICA'S GLOBAL MILITARY BASING NETWORK
U.S. TERRITORIES AND SPECIAL LOCATIONS

	Major	US Military	
	Bases	Personnel	Comments/Major Activities
Guam	10	8,519	B-52s; anti-submarine sound surveillance (SOSUS); nuclear weapons.
Johnston Atoll	1	136	Communications station; chemical weapons storage.
Midway Island	1	13	SOSUS; P-3 anti-submarine warfare (ASW); electronic support--missile tests.
Puerto Rico	6	3,361	Fleet support; sea training range; P-3 ASW planes; main base--Roosevelt Roads.
Marshall Islands	1	42	Kwajalein test range for ABM, ASAT systems; ICBM, SLBM test target area.
Virgin Islands	-	13	Electronic support for naval weapons training; ASW training range.
Wake Island	1	7	Weather station.

FOREIGN AREAS

Antarctica	-	141	Transport and logistics support for scientists in Antarctic Research Program.
Antigua	1	70	Oceanographic research; electronic support for U.S. space and missile testing
Ascension	-	2	Electronic support for space and missile testing; satellite ground station.
Australia	2	753	Satellite naval communications, intelligence; nuclear test detection stations.
Bahamas	-	59	Submarine testing and training; electronic support for missile testing.
Bahrain	-	153	Administrative and logistical support for Navy's Middle East Force.
Bermuda	3	1,844	SOSUS and naval communication stations; P-3 ASW planes; space tracking radar
Cuba	1	2,337	Gunnery and ASW training ranges; minor repair and maintenance facilities.
Diego Garcia	1	1,001	Indian Ocean fleet support; prepositioned supply for possible Persian Gulf war.
Egypt	-	1,468	Medical research unit; hundreds of advisors; large joint exercises every year.
Greenland	2	202	Ballistic missile early warning (EW) radar (Thule); bomber EW radars.
Honduras	-	1,573	Airfield; fuel storage; intelligence facilities; main base: Palmerola.
Japan	31	49,680	Fleet support, repair (Yokosuka); logistics (Sasebo): Marine Division (Okinawa).
Kenya*	-	31	$58M spent--upgrade ports and airfields; peacetime refueling (Mombasa).
Korea, South	41	45,501	Second Infantry Division and 170 combat aircraft; nuclear weapons storage.
Morocco*	-	48	$59M spent to upgrade airfield and fuel storage facilities.
New Zealand	-	59	Black Birch Astronomic Observatory; staging area for Antarctic operations.
Oman*	-	27	$256M spent to improve airfields, ports; $121M for prepositioned equipment.
Panama	5	11,100	Army fortifications; jungle training area; communications station; logistics.
Philippines	11	16,655	Fleet support, repair, ammunition, fuel (Subic Bay); fighter wing (Clark).
Saudia Arabia	-	421	Airborne Warning And Control System (AWACS) aircraft operate from Saudi.
Seychelles	-	4	Air Force satellite tracking, control, and communications station.
Somalia*	-	53	U.S. spent $54 million to upgrade ports and airfields (Mogadishu and Berbera).

NATO AREAS

Belgium	2	3,317	Logistics, air transport--NATO HQ; Communications; nuclear weapons storage
Britain	19	28,497	Missile submarine support; 300 combat aircraft; nuclear weapons storage
Germany, West	224	249,411	Major U.S. Army deployment; 1000s of tanks, 100s of aircraft; nuclear weapons.
Greece	4	3,284	Fleet support (Souda Bay); communications: Hellenikon air base; nuclear weapons.
Iceland	1	3,234	SOSUS; P-3 ASW planes; fighter air defense squadron; main base: Keflavik.
Italy	10	14,829	Fleet support; P-3 ASW planes; nuclear weapons storage.
Netherlands	2	2,872	F-15 fighter wing (Soesterberg); nuclear weapons storage.
Norway	-	1,674	Intelligence gathering facilities; Marine prepositioned equipment (Trondheim).
Portugal	1	1,664	P-3 ASW planes, refueling for trans-Atlantic flights (Lajes Air Base, Azores).
Spain	6	8,724	Fleet support (Rota); P-3 ASW planes; F-16 fighter Wing (relocated to Italy).
Turkey	7	5,034	Intel station--monitor Soviet Navy/missile testing; radars; nuclear weapons.

*These countries do not allow the permanent stationing of U.S. military personnel in peacetime. But the U.S. has financed the improvement of facilities and has been granted special access rights for certain military purposes.

Table 1[1]

Central to the need to reexamine our foreign deployment policy is the fact that the Soviet military threat to Western Europe is gone. Europe maintains a strong conventional war machine without a significant conventional threat to its survival, and is unlikely to be seriously challenged by emerging new threats without warning.

This change affects our force requirements in Asia because it creates a more stable security situation for Japan. Her sea lanes are more secure since the new Commonwealth of Independent States (CIS) dry-docked its navy in early 1989. The cost of operating the CIS fleet and the internal rebuilding of the Russian federation will occupy the CIS for many years to come. Additionally the new CIS seeks the help of Western democracies to rebuild its economic infrastructure. Japan's strong economic capacity and growing military strength make major threats to Japan's survival unlikely for some time.

However, in Asia the threat is uncertain. China is modernizing its military and increasing its arms exports in exchange for hard currency. China along with Brunei, Malaysia, the Philippines, Thailand and Vietnam still dispute the ownership of the Spratly Islands because oil has been found on this chain of islands in the South China Sea. Tensions between India and Pakistan, both already or perhaps soon to be nuclear-armed, continue over the disputed ownership of Kashmir. Furthermore, South Korea's survival may be increasingly threatened by North Korea's recent refusal of International Atomic Energy Agency (IAEA) nuclear safeguards and inspections. North Korea's violation of international arms control regimes and arms export controls make it a threat to South Korea's security.[2]

However, these are regional threats, not global containment issues. Continued decline is forcing North Korea to consider unification either economically on South Korea's terms or militarily on its own terms. It must choose to use or lose its military forces before becoming militarily too weak. China's and the CIS' economic trade with South Korea makes North Korea's predicament more time sensitive and volatile. South

Korea's economic ties with China and the CIS also make it unlikely that these countries will support North Korean aggression.

This reduced threat environment, present and projected, along with the increasing military capability of our allies, allows the U.S. to focus its post-Cold War strategic thinking on the cost of military commitments overseas. The possible threat is now just one element that should be weighed in determining whether Americans must be permanently deployed overseas.

NATO should be re-examined first because historically it is the largest and most expensive example of a successful collective security system and because the threat to both the U.S. and its allies, as well as their defense capabilities, has substantially changed while the cost structure of the alliance has not. Table 2 shows that for the near future, Europe is projected to host most of America's forward deployed troops even though the threat to European security is gone.

NATIONS WITH THE MOST
U.S. TROOPS OVERSEAS

Place	US AID ($ Mil)	Major #Bases 1989	Personnel July 1990	Est. 1995	
* Germany	224		249,411	239,000	150,000
Japan	31		49,680	47,400	
South Korea	41		45,501	40,700	
* Britain	19		28,497	26,400	
* Italy	10		14,829	15,600	
Panama	5		11,100	14,900	
Philippines	11		16,655	13,000	
* Spain	113	6	8,724	7,300	
* Turkey	526	7	5,034	4,800	
* Iceland	1		3,234	3,200	
* Greece	344	4	3,284	2,900	
* Netherlands	2		2,872	2,800	
Cuba	1		2,337	2,600	
* Belgium	2		3,317	2,300	
* Portugal	150	1	1,664	1,600	
Honduras	0		1,573	1,600	
	1,133	365	447,712	426,100	TOTAL
	*1,133	*276	*320,866	*305,900	*TOTAL
	100%	75%	72%	72%	

* Europe/NATO supported countries

Table 2[3]

Many view NATO as the best example of a successful collective security system. In a bipolar world NATO was the linchpin in a global security system. The alliance should receive much of the credit for the fall of the Berlin Wall, the reunification of Germany and the end of the Cold War. After this victory, NATO's continued heavy emphasis on forward U.S. deployment in a multi-polar world suggests it may require fundamental changes apart from its recent decision to perform peacekeeping functions. A clear analysis of the benefits and costs to the United States of our participation in NATO therefore should be made.

Notes

1. NATO areas separated from original and description abbreviated. Sources: DOD, CDI--Chart prepared

Notes

by Center for Defense Information. "The Global Network of United States Military Bases," <u>The Defense Monitor</u>, XVIII, No. 2, (1989), p. 4.

2."Artic to Tropic: Pacific Air Forces poised for Threats" <u>Air Force Times</u> May 3, 1993, p12-13.

3.Chart prepared by the Center for Defense Information. Source: DoD (numbers as of 1989, June 30, 1990, projected)

II. Origin of NATO

Such an examination must begin in the origin and purpose of the NATO alliance (see Appendix 1 for text of treaty). In 1945, the ravages of World War II left Central and Western Europe militarily and economically prostrate and created the Cold War environment. Although Russia was officially an ally, only Canada and the U.S. conducted normal trade with European Countries. The West hoped that the creation of the United Nations (UN) in 1945 would lead to a peaceful world based upon democratic values, human rights, and the rule of law. However, the Soviet Union used the United Nations as a vehicle for spreading its own world vision. The Soviet Union took advantage of the power vacuum in Central Europe, expanding its influence and extending a perimeter to provide a defensive buffer zone for the homeland.

Western European countries, viewing the expanding Russian defensive perimeter as a threat to their survival, expected the United States would immediately want to help. However, the impression left by Secretary of State Robert A. Lovett during the first five meetings of the Seven-Power Ambassadors was that the U.S. was only interested in learning what steps the Europeans were taking for themselves. Such a response harkened back to this country's 150 year-historical aversion to entering into entangling alliances.[4]

American caution about alliances sprang from Washington's warning to all future presidents of the perils involved with permanent agreements: "[t]aking care always to keep ourselves, by suitable establishments, on a respectable defensive posture, we may safely trust to temporary alliances for extraordinary emergencies." He warned that "[t]here can be no greater error than to expect, or calculate upon real favours from nation to nation. 'T is an illusion which experience must cure, which a just pride ought to discard."[5] Washington urged the country to avoid permanent alliances that would threaten American interests. Washington's prescription might well see NATO as a temporary alliance structure that has fulfilled its purpose.

American presidents for almost a century and a half followed Washington's advice. They traditionally sought to avoid European conflicts and military commitments, World War I and World War II being the exceptions that proved the rule. The decision to create NATO represented a major departure from this policy.[6]

After World War II, the U.S. government created two entities to secure American interests in Europe. President Truman approved the Marshall Plan to rebuild the European economy and helped create NATO to defend the governments and economy of Europe against Soviet expansionism. Both were created for an emergency and expected to be only temporary in nature. Truman also recognized that Europe served as our best market outlet. American industries were producing at maximum capacity after the war, and needed markets, but the world's most sophisticated markets were nations that could no longer afford to house, feed, or defend themselves. President Truman launched the Marshall Plan in this context, largely because it satisfied American interests. While the Marshall Plan turned out to be only a temporary solution, NATO became permanent.

Motivations for NATO

The primary reasons for the United States' signing of the North Atlantic Treaty (see Appendix 1) were to contain Soviet aggression, to provide the peacemaking envisioned for the United Nations and to deter aggression. Promoting collective self-defense as modeled by the Rio Pact and ensuring self-help and mutual aid among regional members of security pacts were deemed a prerequisite by Congress for U.S. participation.[7]

Deterrence was a major reason for the creation of NATO. The United States wanted to contribute to the maintenance of peace by making clear its determination to exercise the right of individual or collective self-defense under Article 51 of the UN charter. The United States originally desired to maintain complete freedom of action. Its purpose was to avoid any direct alliance while encouraging like-minded members to cooperate among themselves for national security reasons. Consistent with Article 51, the U.S. wanted to maximize its efforts "to provide the United Nations with armed forces as contemplated by the charter, and to obtain agreement among member Nations upon universal regulation and reduction of armaments under adequate and dependable guarantee against violation."[8]

In reaffirming the policy to achieve international peace and security through the UN, the U.S. enunciated a foreign policy that increasingly placed the country at loggerheads with the Soviet Union. Soviet vetoes served as proof of differing world visions between the U.S. and Russia.[9] The U.S. wanted to overcome the Russian vetoes on questions dealing with the peaceful settlement of a wide variety of issues including the addition or recognition of new members favorable to its view to the United Nations.

Pre-requisites for U.S. Participation

Consistent with the intent of the Rio Pact, the U.S. sought to promote collective self-defense while avoiding arbitrary or automatic commitments. The U.S. encouraged progressive development of regional and other collective arrangements for self-defense in accordance with the rules of the UN. The U.S. sought to integrate its own national security with others in the hope that such arrangements would ultimately enhance our own security. There was to be no open-ended obligations of any sort to provide military assistance to Western Europe.[10] In fact, the original reason for defining a North Atlantic region was to serve as protection for U.S. interests.

Self-help and mutual aid were the principles under which the United States would associate itself with regional and other collective security treaties. Americans expected a large European commitment to mutual aid and self-help before these countries received U.S. help. They also expected that Europeans would eventually provide for their own defense. Therefore, if an alliance's survival was deemed to have a vital effect upon the national security of the United States, and if the other members helped each other, then the United States desired participation. Dean Acheson's view was that "no individual country was supposed to be getting a meal ticket from anybody else."[11] The United States would not become the sole supporter of such an organization. Each participant country would have to continually demonstrate its will or ability to help itself first.

Clearly, Americans participated in the creation of NATO along with alliance participants who were to maintain a foundation of self-help and mutual aid. There were to be no arbitrary or automatic U.S. commitments. However, the limitations to U.S. NATO participation were subsequently forgotten.

After World War II, the U.S. was determined to stand against aggression. America wanted global military force reductions and desired the UN to be the world's mechanism for making peace. Previous American attempts to promote peace, democracy and the rule of law through the United Nations had been blocked by Russian vetoes in the Security Council. To counter the UN stalemate, the U.S. Senate Foreign Relations Committee passed the Vandenberg resolution which set up the pre-requisites by which the U.S. would support the creation of NATO. The lessons of World War I and II seemed to indicate that the only way to prevent the horrors of another world war was to take immediate and effective measures against those who threaten the peace. The United States would need to find a way, without violating its obligations to the UN, to stop future aggression. U.S. participation in NATO was that solution. NATO could act as a deterrent while the United States rescued Europe with the Marshall Plan. The U.S. assumed that it was cheaper to arm our allies than actually fight and, once armed, the Europeans would increasingly take care of their own needs.[12]

A Fundamentally Different NATO Today

Today, absent a threat to its survival, NATO's purpose is unclear. The danger posed by the former Soviet Union has receded and even though the military potential of Russia is still great, Russia's hostile intention is far from determined. The Warsaw Pact no longer exists as a cogent unit with large conventional forces massed at the German gates to Western Europe.

With the strategic satellite warning system in existence today, it is a very remote possibility that any threat to the survival of the United States or Europe would go undetected without several months or years of warning. United States strategic space collection processes allow U.S. leadership the time to assess and react to potential new threats if necessary. In addition the new generation of U.S. technology, such as the Stealth B-2 bomber, offer the promise of reacting to any threat in the world within hours.

With this current threat assessment, NATO has redefined for itself a new mission apart from its original purpose as supported by the American people. NATO members, individually possessing different means and national interests, could only reach consensus on peacekeeping as the new mission. Members refused to adopt peacemaking as the NATO mission. "Peacekeeping, a role the U.N. has played over the years, . . . involves monitoring and enforcing a cease-fire agreement agreed to by two or more former combatants"[13] while military peacemaking which means "action to bring hostile parties to agreement, essentially through peaceful means such as those foreseen in Chapter VI' of the U.N. Charter . . . is synonymous with the American concept of peace-enforcement. . ."[14] The lowest common denominator for agreement on a new mission was that NATO would restructure itself for three levels of rapid deployment for peacekeeping missions. The new mission as defined does not include peacemaking missions.[15]

NATO countries have been internally focused on regional European matters since World War II. It is unlikely, with the risks and costs that go along with global peacemaking, that NATO countries, given their differences in capabilities and resources, would automatically plan and participate in superpower responsibilities. Thus, NATO may only have been able to agree among all participant countries to the peacekeeping role which implies a limited risk and response.

NATO's resources can automatically be used for peacekeeping missions of

European member states, but require committee approval for crises not directly related to European security matters. Central and Eastern European security problems may not receive attention by NATO.[16] If a new threat emerges that does not directly threaten the security of a European country, the member's first position is to let some other entity like the United States or United Nations respond first. If such entities contain the new threat and belligerent parties request a peacekeeping force, NATO may then respond. This means that the U.S. will have to respond unilaterally or gather coalition support from individual NATO countries if it chooses to engage in peacemaking operations in Central and Eastern Europe, areas that include such "hot-spots" as Bosnia.

NATO's new mission will cost the U.S. more for tightly focused Western European security concerns because NATO does not possess the necessary airlift capabilities to respond with heavy equipment. The NATO peacekeeping mission now requires additional permanent strategic airlift forces that were not required for the classical fixed European battle to support the more mobile mission of peacekeeping.[17] Traditional European scenarios prepositioned armor and heavy equipment. Future NATO peacekeeping missions will need the capability to move NATO heavy assets to where they are needed. Reforger exercises in the past have used U.S.-based strategic lift assets to simulate deployments to Europe. NATO now requires more European-based strategic airlift than it possesses to respond quickly to its new peacekeeping mission and it is not apparent how NATO countries will obtain the necessary strategic airlift resources.

The failure of European countries to reach consensus in NATO or take a greater role in Central and Eastern Europe security issues will force the U.S. to develop employment options outside of NATO's politics to respond to global contingencies. Developing this flexibility will cost the U.S. more money.

Simply put, American troops deployed to Europe are more difficult to redeploy to Asia. Whether the U.S. is responding in the Gulf, Europe or worldwide, NATO bureaucratic procedures and politics limit the speed and flexibility of U.S. response with forces permanently positioned in Europe. Several examples will be explored later to demonstrate current trends in U.S.-European affairs. Additionally NATO's new peacekeeping mission is not necessarily of vital interest to the United States. Peacekeeping in Europe ought to be a European-sponsored activity if U.S. interests are only remotely threatened.

NATO's search for a new mission to justify its existence underscores the point that the U.S. presence in Europe was not designed to be permanent. The 1949 alignment of U.S. and European security interests was real. Today such an alignment is illusory. At that time the presence of U.S. troops was not envisioned, and when eventually required, was not intended to last past the time Europe could defend itself. In the 1949 Senate hearings on North Atlantic security, Senator Bourne Hickenlooper of Iowa asked: will the United States "be expected to send substantial numbers of troops [to Europe] as a more or less permanent contribution to the development of [West Europe's] capacity to resist [Soviet aggression]?"[18] "The answer to that question," replied Secretary of State Dean Acheson, "is a clear and absolute No [emphasis present in text]"[19] "More or less permanent" is hard to define, but the United States still plans to maintain (53 years later) 100,000 soldiers in Europe at a tremendous continuing cost to American taxpayers.

European Defense And Arms Exports

Unlike 1949, most NATO countries today are capable of providing for their own defense. Most countries hosting U.S. troops have the economic prosperity, manpower, and industry to defend themselves. European members of NATO have a collective GNP greater than that of the U.S. and at least 4-5 times that of the former Soviet Union, yet America spends more on NATO defenses than the other 15 alliance members combined.[20] The original U.S. drafters founded NATO on the premise that European countries would have to help themselves before America would help, yet the United

States still provides over a billion dollars in military aid to the poorest NATO countries: Turkey, Greece, Spain and Portugal.[21] The United States continued support of NATO today suggests that the security of Europe as a whole means more to the U.S. then to each European country individually. European countries have sufficient manpower resources to defend themselves in this reduced threat environment. America's European NATO allies collectively have more than 3 million active-duty troops drawn from a combined population of almost 400 million (87 million males aged 15-49)(2.6 million/year reach draft age excluding Britain and Iceland).[22] Germany alone has a population of 78 million, with a military force that numbers almost 600,000 (to be reduced to 370,000 by 1994). If needed Germany has 17 million males ages 15-49 available for military service; every year over 418,000 German males reach military age.[23] Under the principle of mutual aid and self-help, Europeans have vast untapped manpower for collective self-defense.

Europe also has the ability to manufacture and support the high technology weapons that it needs. France, Britain, Germany and Italy--powerful industrialized countries that are among the world's 10 leading exporters of weapons--are capable of manufacturing in quantity most of the weapons necessary to satisfy their own requirements.[24]

European capability for creating high technology weapons also allows them to contribute to future threats in unstable third world regions. While the U.S. also exports weapons, it involves itself in the solution to global threats. The difference is responsibility for one's actions; U.S. global interests make it more likely that Americans will respond before other Western nations to stabilize third world tensions when the need arises. Many Western countries sold military materials to India and Pakistan. When tensions between India and Pakistan erupted in 1991, the U.S. responded diplomatically to encourage confidence building measures--thus India and Pakistan agreed not to attack each other's growing nuclear infrastructure--which lowered regional tensions.

The Gulf crisis provides an example when Americans responded before Europeans to a third world threat caused in part by Western sales of military arms. Many western countries including the United States sold weapons, equipment, and technology that supported the Iraqi war machine. Over 100 German companies are under indictment under German law for exporting arms to Saddam Hussein.[25] In effect, the western desire to maintain a high technology defense industrial base requires weapons exports to keep production lines open for one's own use, but has future implications for future world threats.

France, one the most aggressive European arms exporting countries, sold India its original nuclear reactor and continues today to sell ballistic missile technology that India claims to be using in its peaceful space launch vehicle (SLV) program. India routinely rotates its engineers and scientists from its civil space launch vehicle program and its military ballistic missile programs. Technologies between SLVs and ballistic missiles are almost identical. The result of western help is that India, which exploded its first nuclear device in 1974, has developed the operational Agni intermediate range ballistic missile and is very close to completing an ICBM. Thus, not only are Europeans capable of developing their own weapons, their export of this capability has increased the instability of many third world regions, creating new threats to which the United States may someday feel compelled to respond.

The principle upon which NATO was originally founded--continued mutual aid and self-help before American help--seems to have been forgotten. American presence in Europe was intended to be a temporary emergency measure for security. Today, U.S. forces seem likely to remain even though NATO countries possess the innate ability to defend themselves.

Notes

4. U.S. Secretary of State Lovett attended the first five meetings of the Seven-Power Ambassadors' Committee held between 6 and 9 July held to decide what to do about the Soviet threat to the West and the determination of the West to withstand future threats. It was held against during the blockade of Berlin and Western Air Lift. p34-37.
Sir Nicholas Henderson, The Birth of NATO, (Boulder, CO: Westview Press, Inc., 1983), p. 37.

5. Washington's Farewell Address, Webster's First Bunker Hill Oration, Lincoln's Gettysburg Address, ed. by Charles Robert Gaston, (Boston: Ginn and Company, 1919), p. 17.

6. Sir Nicholas Henderson, The Birth of NATO, (Boulder, CO: Westview Press, Inc., 1983), p. 19-20.

7. The "Rio Pact" was a set of principles used in South America to promote security cooperation. Senator Vandenberg used the Rio Pact as model in his speech, June 13, 1945, at the UN Conference at San Francisco to sell his concept for European security cooperation. Senator Vandenberg, in the formal part of the language of the report of the Foreign Relations Committee said the Pact would accomplish the following: "(1) it imposes an obligation on the contracting parties to take positive action to assist in meeting armed attack against any American state; (2) it provides for consultation and action, not only in the event of armed attacks and other acts of aggression but whenever any other fact or situation might endanger the peace of the Americas; (3) it outlines the machinery and organs of consultation which the American states will utilize in taking collective security measures to meet such threats; (4) it defines a special hemispheric security area; (5) it enumerates the political, economic, and military measures which may be taken against an aggressor; and (6) it provides for the effective integration of inter-American peace machinery into the United Nations". The Private Papers of Senator Arthur H. Vandenberg, ed. by Arthur H. Vandenberg Jr.,(Cambridge: The Riverside Press, 1952), p. 366-7.

8. Hearings before the Committee on Foreign Relations on the Vandenberg Resolution and the North Atlantic Treaty, 80th Cong., 2nd Sess., S. Res. 239 and 81st Cong., 1st Sess., Executive L, (Washington: U.S. Government Printing Office, 1973), p. 3.

9. Ibid. p. 2.

10. Ibid., p. 1. During the Executive Session the Chairman, Senator Arthur H. Vandenberg stated: "In connection with the defense for Western Europe, we were seeking most emphatically to avoid any arbitrary or automatic commitments, and to largely proceed on the same theory, that upon which we built the European recovery program, namely, that anything contemplated by us should be at our option as a result of the activities of these beneficiary countries in Europe which might integrate their own security efforts in a fashion which would invite some sort of cooperation on our part in our own interest."

11. Ibid., p. 99.

12. Ibid., p. 217.

13. Donald M. Snow, Peacekeeping, Peacemaking and Peace-Enforcement: The U.S. Role in the New International Order, (Strategic Studies Institute, Feb. 1993), p. 4.

14. This form, which might be designated as military peacemaking, is synonymous with the American concept of peace-enforcement and is clearly more difficult, if more relevant. The problems with peace-enforcement are difficult for at least four obvious and preliminary reasons, each of which interact to make entrance into peace-enforcement an adventure to be undertaken only with extreme caution. At this point, these difficulties are introduced to illustrate the problems. The differences between peacekeeping and

peace-enforcement are expanded in the next section.

First, there is the nature of the situations for which military peacemaking may be deemed relevant. Normally, they will reflect deep-seated animosities with historical, ethnic, religious and other hatreds that layer upon one another as countries are torn apart and regenerated. The problems that underlay the violence that is to be suppressed are political and ultimately solvable only through political agreements that cannot be imposed by outsiders. Imposed cease-fires may be the precondition to negotiate political settlements; since the absence of ability or interest in negotiating is why fighting is occurring, it is hard to know where effectively to enter and break the vicious circle.

Second, the fact that peacemakers are needed suggests that one or more opponents to conflict do not desire peace more than the continuation of war. What this means is that the peacemakers are likely to be unwelcome by some or all of those on whom they seek to enforce peace. This certainly will make the peace enforcer's job more difficult. Both (or all) of the combatants may be attacking the peacemakers as well as one another; the analogy to a policeman intervening in a domestic dispute may be appropriate. It is not clear, for instance, that an international peacemaking force sent to create a cease-fire in Bosnia and Herzegovina would be greeted with anything but a hail of Serbian bullets.

Third, peacemaking may require troops with some specialized capabilities beyond those of peacekeepers, such as considerably more offensive capability and more political sophistication to recognize potential unintended effects of their actions. These forces will presumable have to fight their way into the combat zone and, in some cases, use force physically to separate the combatants. As such, they will be called upon to engage in offensive actions where mistaken action can worsen the situation. Moreover, they will likely inflict and suffer casualties, possibly making them less welcome and undercutting domestic support back home for their activities. The requirements of the Weinberger Doctrine - to the degree its precepts remain relevant - could well be challenged as operations unfold.

Quite obviously, these forces will have to be equipped and trained differently, and they will have to be considerable larger and more capable than conventional peacekeepers. To provide competent peace enforcers will require special skills for the troops (for instance, negotiating and foreign language competence), and provision of adequate firepower and defensive capability to protect themselves from hostile action by those they seek to help. Given these factors, they must also be prepared for a level of ingratitude from the target population of which the Vietnam experience is only a faint reflection.

Moreover, peace-enforcement will be much more costly than peacekeeping or diplomatic peacemaking. Certainly U.N resources are inadequate for such actions, which may explain why the Secretary General adopts a much more modest and inexpensive conception of peacemaking. Diplomatic peacemaking, in other words, may be all the U.N. can undertake realistically. It will thus fall to the participating peace enforcer nations to pick up the tab: Out of whose budgets will the money come?

Fourth, peace-enforcement will not solve the underlying problems in most areas of potential application. It may have been possible in 1992 to impose a peace in Bosnia and Herzegovina through the insertion of adequate force, but a cease-fire so imposed would not address the underlying animosities. Since the peace enforcers will eventually leave, the problems may simply revert after their departure. Peace enforcers, in other words, had better be prepared for disappointments after their part of the operation is concluded. They may be able to create conditions favorable for follow-on peacekeepers in some instances; in other situations, they may not. Put another way, a short-term objective-convoying food in Somalia- may be easily achievable. The long-term objective - a stable authority in that country -may not be.

Boutros-Ghali adds peacekeeping, which he defines as "the deployment of a United Nations presence in the field, hitherto with the consent of all the parties concerned, involving United Nations military and/or police personnel and frequently civilians as well. Peace-keeping is a technique that expands the possibility for both the prevention of conflict and the making of peace."

This definition expands the concept in a dangerous way. Traditional peacekeeping was feasible because two conditions adhered before peacekeepers were inserted: fighting had ceased, and both or all parties preferred the presence of the peacekeepers to their absence (the peacekeepers are invited guests). Under those circumstances, the prototypical peacekeeper arose: the lightly armed, defensively oriented observer force that physically separated former combatants and observed their adherence to the cease-fire while negotiations for peace occurred.

The danger is in thinking peacekeeping forces can be inserted into peace-enforcement situations; that somehow represent a lineal extension of one another. Peace-enforcement requires, as argued, very different forces qualitatively and quantitatively than does peacekeeping. The result of confusing roles and forces has been most evident in the placing of the UNPROFOR peacekeepers in a war zone in Sarajevo, where the peacekeepers were placed in a peace-enforcement situation and have proven--unsurprisingly--not to be up to a task for which they are unprepared.

Donald M. Snow, <u>Peacekeeping, Peacemaking and Peace-Enforcement: The U.S. Role in the New International Order</u>, (Strategic Studies Institute, Feb. 1993), p. 16-19.

Boutros Boutros-Ghali, <u>An Agenda for Peace: Preventive Diplomacy, Peacemaking, and Peace-Keeping</u>, (New York: United Nations, 1992), p. 11, 20-27.

15. I discovered the limits and capabilities of NATO's new agreed upon mission in a personal interview with Colonel Michael A. Caine, USAF, State Defense Exchange Officer, Department of State, Bureau of European Affairs, Office of European Affairs--Regional Politico-Military Affairs in room 6515 on December 15, 1992. NATO's new mission area was confirmed in personal interview with Commander Michael N. Pocalyko, USN, Senior Fellow, The Atlantic Council of the United States, 1616 H Street, N.W. Washington D.C. on December 16, 1992. A recent article confirms the new NATO three response level missions: Charles Miller, "NATO Unveils Rapid Reaction Corps," <u>Defense News</u>, Oct. 5, 1992.

16."The U.S. as the World's Policeman? Ten Reasons to Find a Different Role," <u>The Defense Monitor</u>, XX, No. 1, (1991), p. 8.

Charles Miller, "NATO Unveils Rapid Reaction Corps," <u>Defense News</u>, (Oct. 5, 1992), p. 12.

Andrew Weinschenk, "Galvin Calls for NATO Preeminence," <u>Defense Week</u>, (June 8, 1992), p. 8.

17.Colonel Michael A. Caine, personal interview, U. S. Department of State, Washington D.C., Dec. 15, 1992.

Theresa Hitchens, "NATO Forum To Focus On Peacekeeping Duty," <u>Defense News</u>, (Nov. 23, 1992), p. 8.

Theresa Hitchens, "NATO Meeting Will Feature Peacekeeping in E. Europe," <u>Defense News</u>, (Oct. 26, 1992), p. 26.

Charles Miller, "NATO Unveils Rapid Reaction Corps," <u>Defense News</u>, (Oct. 5, 1992), p. 12.

18.Sir Nicholas Henderson, <u>The Birth of NATO</u>, (Boulder, CO: Westview Press, Inc., 1983), p. 38.

19.Dean Acheson, <u>Present At The Creation: My Years in the State Department</u>, (New York: W. W. Norton & Company, 1969), p. 285.

20."The U. S. as the World's Policeman? Ten Reasons to Find a Different Role," <u>The Defense Monitor</u>, XX, No. 1, (1991), p. 4.

21.Hearings before the Committee on Foreign Relations on the Vandenberg Resolution and the North Atlantic Treaty, 80th Cong., 2nd Sess., S. Res. 239 and 81st Cong., 1st Sess., Executive L, (Washington: U.S. Government Printing Office, 1973).

<u>A Statement of Policy to be Followed in the U. N.</u>, p. 5.

Secretary Lovett: This is a statement policy, as I understand it, to be followed by the United States, within the United Nations, wherever the national security of this country involves association by constitutional processes with other groups of countries who have banded together for collective security, and where self-help and mutual aid are a condition precedent to any such association.

<u>The Merit of the Resolution</u>, p. 29.

Notes

The Chairman: My answer to you, Senator Wiley, would be this: In connection with the reestablishment of Europe as a going concern, that being recognized as highly important to our own national security, we have proceeded on the economic front, and the question still remains as to whether or not you can proceed successfully on the economic front in the presence of total insecurity in the area, or fears of insecurity.

It is perfectly obvious that we are to be assaulted with demands for direct military assistance or alliance. We are already hearing that demand from some sections. It is perfectly clear that we are being assailed, and are going to be even more assailed in the future, by demands for the old lend-lease technique in respect to security, and from my point of view we cannot yield to that sort of an approach.

But in my point of view, if we can find a way to offer a security encouragement which is adequate to the situation and which is completely in line with our own national security requirements, it is highly useful to us to do it.

Does this move in that direction? I think it does, for the following reasons: If we can completely meet this situation by simply pointing out to Western Europe that if it wants to create a self-help defensive unitary entity within the charter and under the terms of the charter, and if it can succeed in proving to us that it means business in connection with it, we not only encourage that objective but if, as and when it is achieved we are prepared to consider in what degree we wish, in the name of our national security, to associate ourselves with that enterprise.

I think the great gain to us on the one hand is that we have moved forward into the field of security without involving ourselves in any permanent obligations of any nature; second, that by so moving we have provided a complete answer to those who are going to constantly press for far greater movements in this direction, and we must have an affirmative answer. We cannot rest entirely on the negative answer.

Third, fundamentally and philosophically, so far as I am concerned, we are pointing out that there is inherent in this charter a way for like-minded member nations to implement article 51 in respect to collective self-defense entirely outside of the jurisdiction of the veto.

Chart prepared by the Center for Defense Information. Source: DoD (numbers as of 1989, June 30, 1990, projected) see Table 2.

22."The U.S. as the World's Policeman? Ten Reasons to Find a Different Role," The Defense Monitor, XX, No. 1, (1991), p. 4.

23.Ibid.

24.Ibid.

25.Specific information about the identity of the German companies involved or the goods sold to Iraq are tightly controlled under German Law until after the German company is tried. All 100 cases can be verified, but not in an unclassified manner.

III. What Do We Get For Our Money

Some features of the United States forward deployment policy remain useful to the U.S. in the new world order. Access to foreign bases in Europe, interoperable military equipment, joint training, and direct military lines of communications with European nations have always been helpful. Now however, the undoubted utility of these aspects must be measured against the problems they entail. Even disregarding cost---a not inconsiderable concern as we shall see---all of these ancillary capabilities have significant problems.

One such asset is having access to foreign bases to stage aircraft in an emergency. Access to foreign bases, maintained by host governments, can be useful when national security interests are shared among coalition partners. As Desert Storm illustrated, however, if the U.S. desired access to European bases it must first ask each foreign country individually for approval. NATO did not in the context of Operation Desert Storm provide automatic help to the U.S.-led coalition.

Interoperability of military equipment is a valuable feature of the U.S. participation in NATO. Supporting the logistics coalition of forces is easier if each side uses standard sustainment. Using the 7.62mm NATO ammunition is one successful example where using multi-national forces can be supported by the same logistical source.

Acquiring interoperable military equipment should continue as long as there are bilateral incentives to do so. In the past, some NATO interoperability efforts have been less than successful because of political pressures for each country to manufacture its own equipment disregarding such criteria as cost and comparative effectiveness. This issue works in both directions. Just as the Europeans may prefer to "buy European", the U.S. may decide to buy American systems to maintain American production lines. This will complicate the issue of interoperability regardless of the American role in NATO.

Interoperability will be further threatened as individual countries protect their newest technology and thus prefer to buy at home. The U.S. protects its stealth technology, some satellite hardware, and other technologies thought to represent a relative advantage over a potential aggressor. The British build better minesweepers and destroyers than the U.S. and the German Leopard II tank is arguably better than the U.S. M-1 Abrams tank, but the U.S. continues to purchase American systems.[26] For similar reasons the new European fighter will probably be more expensive, less interoperable with U.S. hardware, and less capable than the most advanced U.S. fighter, but will be bought by Europe for economic reasons. The trend to buy internally will further undermine one of the key motivations for keeping NATO.

Joint training and exercises are very valuable for both U.S. and foreign troops. Although expensive, they allow each country to become accustomed to each other's methods. If the United States were to withdraw forces from NATO, it would be worthwhile to fund and conduct joint deployment exercises with potential coalition partners every two or three years. The scope and scale of the NATO Reforger exercise provided basic skills and training for U.S. logistics personnel. They relied upon some of this experience to deploy and sustain U.S. troops in Operation Desert Shield/Storm. Joint training is perhaps an unambiguous benefit.

Face-to-face military communications with the highest ranking foreign military officers is valued by senior American military leaders.[27] These meetings provide U.S. officers an unfiltered channel of communication as opposed to normal bureaucratic diplomatic and commercial channels. Long-term military relationships can foster trust and mutual respect; however, the "up-or-out" system of military promotions at the highest level may see many senior officers retire from active duty before the real benefits from military relationships are realized.

Ambassador H. Allen Holmes, former Assistant Secretary of State for Politico-

Military Affairs and present Ambassador at Large for Burden Sharing, believes that the primary advantage of NATO to the U.S. resides in this integrated politico-military structure. He believes that the extra military communications channels, interoperable equipment, common procedures, and joint training are all positive aspects of NATO not found in any other permanent organization.

Ambassador Holmes used Operation Desert Storm to make his case. Although Desert Storm was not a NATO operation, it was the established command and control structure that allowed the transshipment of war materials from Rotterdam, Europe's largest port, to the Gulf in record time. The established NATO command and control infrastructure more easily allowed the priority shipping and handling of military related exports be transported to the Gulf.[28] Ambassador Holmes believes that NATO's integrated politico-military structure is unique in the world.

Without a military threat, maintaining political influence and economic access in Europe through our role in NATO become major reasons to keep American soldiers deployed in Europe. If this is so, then our forward-based troops legitimize the process in the eyes of the foreign host governments. Without a physical presence, U.S. leadership would carry little weight in addressing chiefly European concerns. Theoretically U.S. presence makes our access to overseas trade, sea lanes and other communications easier and provides a measure of security or guaranteed stability for United States' investment.

One military organizational argument says that if the services bring the forces home, Congressional cuts in the military could be higher than if forces remained overseas. Historically, after major conflicts like Desert Storm, the requirement for large trained and equipped ground forces disappears from public support. This usually leaves the U.S. Army understrength and unprepared for the next conflict. With a diminished world threat, the U.S. population is unlikely to desire the entire Army back in the U.S. for coastal defense. In reality, forward deployment has assuaged concerns about a standing army. If much of the Army is not kept overseas, then political pressures might force greater Army size reductions and impact readiness. With present high technology weaponry, the U.S. Army would need months or years to rebuild a large modern force when necessary.

Former Secretary of Defense Dick Cheney, Chairman of the Joint Chiefs Colin Powell, and NATO Commander General John Galvin assert that the United States needs to maintain forces deployed to contain new emerging threats called "instability, uncertainty and unpredictability" in Europe.[29] Basically their argument is that U.S. cooperation provides for deterrence and regional stability much more effectively than could individual nations' efforts, through effective sharing of defense burdens and responsibilities. It also establishes America as Europe's guardian when European problems may have little bearing on U.S. interests.

Another argument for keeping U.S. forces in Europe is to avoid the creation of a power vacuum which would hypothetically be filled by France, the United Kingdom or Germany. U.S. troops in Europe obviate the need for substantial local defense efforts, thus providing the balance between these three traditional partners. Essentially the argument is the allies cannot be trusted to defend themselves from either internal or external threats and the rise of any single nation will bring conflict rather than stability.

Problems with NATO

The unique qualities of NATO do not always translate into more effective military operations for the U.S. Even postulating a need for continued U.S. presence in Europe and granting the value of some aspects of forward deployment, there are still associated problems with pursuing American foreign policy with NATO resources. U.S. policy options can be impaired if the security issues do not directly or immediately align with European interests. The real question remains whether the U.S. would have unencumbered access to her security assets when needed because U.S. forces are stationed in Europe primarily to defend NATO's direct interests. Any time the U.S. requires the use of European-based troops and equipment or the use of NATO bases for other than NATO's direct interest, the U.S. might find itself looking for alternatives, because NATO-committed assets are by custom not necessarily available for wider American interests.

Having a large force forward deployed in Europe reduces U.S. flexibility for meeting out-of-NATO contingencies. The U.S. had to ask each NATO ally individually to guarantee U.S. access to U.S. NATO facilities supporting Operation Desert Storm. Use of U.S. equipment positioned in Europe was not guaranteed. Alternatively, support for the first deployed units in Operation Desert Shield/Storm was supplied by prepositioned stocks from Army and USAF Afloat Prepositioning Ships (APS), Marine Corps Maritime Prepositioning Squadron (MPS) vessels, and air deployable packages of war reserve material (WRM).[30] The U.S. decision to fund and develop a prepositioning program for the different regions of the world proved in the Gulf to be a valuable means to improve combat capability and responsiveness.

A second out-of-area example shows a similar constraint on U.S. response that cost the U.S. flexibility. The U.S. was forced to provide limited range carrier air support to American humanitarian efforts to supply food and medicine to Bosnia in 1993. Italy denied U.S. access to NATO bases for fighter escort that were closer and would have allowed longer coverage and thus required fewer sorties in the area of interest. The Italians provided other support for the operation but would not allow American armed escorts to stage from their bases.[31] Future uses of U.S. equipment and forces already in Europe may require diplomatic discussions before action.

Negotiations with our Allies can be a major problem. NATO is unlikely to participate in out-of-NATO operations at significant cost or risk to itself. For example,

NATO help was not the first help the United States received in Operation Desert Shield/Storm. American diplomats had to negotiate with European allies to use NATO resources against Iraq even though Europe is arguably more dependent on stability in the Middle East and assured access to oil. The process of having to negotiate with our allies for help during a conflict can cost the U.S. valuable time and flexibility. With the U.S. downsizing its forces, this lack of flexibility will worsen or be even more damaging in the future.

Today's threats and possible challenges require U.S. military forces capable of rapid deployment, intervention, and unilateral police action in "trouble spots" anywhere in the world. The question is whether the United States can be more reliable and efficient with or without NATO. The gap between U.S. and NATO interests may be widening given the recent examples. And whatever benefits accrue from continued participation, many can argue that the cost of NATO membership is high, and may no longer be the best expenditure of a shrinking defense dollar.

Notes

26. Anthony J. Watts, ed., Jane's Underwater Warfare Systems 1992-1993 (Virginia: Jane's Data Division, 1992), p. 232-239.
Christopher F. Foss, ed., Jane's Armour and Artillery 1992-1993 (Virginia: Jane's Data Division, 1992), p. 53-64, 141-159.

27. Ambassador H. Allen Holmes, personal interview in Washington D.C., Dec. 1992.

28. Ambassador H. Allen Holmes, personal interview in Washington D.C., Dec. 1992.

29. John Lancaster, "Top General Supports 150,000 U. S. Troops in Europe as Hedge," The Washington Post,(Mar. 4, 1992), p. A20.
Rowan Scarborough, "Germany wants to keep U.S. Troops in Europe," The Washington Times, (March 5, 1992) p. A6.
Cable News Network Interview with JCS Chairman Gen Colin Powell, Nov. 25, 1991.

30. "Appendix F1-F80, Logistics Build Up and Sustainment" Title V Report, Conduct of Persian Gulf War, Final Report to Congress (DOD April 1992)

Notes

31. Briefing May 1993 from ACSC Major Jim Brooks. He was sent to Europe to view and report on JFACC operations of Operation Provide Hope.

IV. Cost Analysis

The benefits the U.S. receives for its participation in defense alliances may not be worth the cost. During the '80s the U.S. spent $150 billion per year to protect European countries and about $40 billion per year to protect parts of Asia.[32] As the FY 1993 U.S. defense budget was being reduced, DoD estimated that it still spent about 50 percent of its total budget for Europe.[33]

None of our forces are manned, equipped or organized for only one theater of operations.[34] For example, deployment of the U.S. VII Corps from Europe to Southwest Asia during Operation Desert Storm is a clear example of the multiple contingency concept. Table 1 (page 2) shows major U.S. overseas bases available to support contingencies.[35] In light of our ongoing and future planned force reductions, most U.S. forces will have to be available for use in other regional contingencies.

FY93 Military Spending Outlays (Billions)[36]

Department of Defense	$278
Department of Energy nuclear weapons	$13
"National Defense" subtotal	$291
*Military share of interest on the debt	$79
*Veterans	$34
*Military aid	$7
Military NASA, Coast Guard, etc	$5
TOTAL	$ 416
* Potential NATO/Europe related expenses	

Table 3

Government costs associated with military spending may not include all of the related expenses. An argument can be made that some portion of the interest paid on the U.S. debt attributed to defense spending, cost of benefits for veterans stationed primarily overseas, and cost of military aid paid to foreign countries should be represented, but are not shown as part of the DOD budget. Table 3 estimates these costs for FY 1993.

Congress makes it increasingly difficult for the Pentagon to justify annual budget. If U.S. participation in NATO were to be reduced, it is likely that some portion of the U.S. force structure in NATO would be eliminated while other portions based upon mission and threat could be redeployed. Congress' formula for calculating what NATO costs the U.S. recently put the expense of NATO at $150 billion per year (see Table 4). However, DoD internal FY 92 data shows a range of costs from under $5 billion to around $50 billion, depending on the assumptions used. The Pentagon argues that more meaningful and analytically sound methodologies to identify the budget impacts of our forces in Europe, or to measure the incremental costs of forward deployments, yield lower figures. Although the true cost is probably below the Congress reported cost of $150 billion, it is most likely above DoD's figure of $50 billion.[37]

When the threat to the survival of Europe was real, the Pentagon did not need to link specific NATO missions with costs because for almost fifty years NATO has been used to justify most of the Defense Department's expenditures regardless of the real reason for the acquisition. Few challenged this method when the Soviet threat was immediate and real. Today, that primary threat is gone and the Defense Department's methods of justifying the cost of its requirements have not yet evolved into a new system accepted by the United States' people or Congress. NATO has served our security interests extremely well in the past, but that may not be true in the future.[38]

Unavailable.

Table 4 Cost components US Force NATO[39]

What Does NATO Really Cost Us?

The real cost of NATO is over $100 billion a year as shown in Table 5. The average yearly cost per soldier, fully equipped in Europe, is about $58,800.[40] Given the July 1990 figures for numbers of soldiers in Europe from Table 2, that's $17.99 billion. U.S. military aid to NATO countries from Table 2 adds another $1.13 billion. Given

----
NATO/Europe Forward Deployment Costs
*Estimated Cost (Billions)

1. 305,900 x $58,800/soldier **= $17.99
2. Military Aid= $ 1.13
3. O&M cost 75% x $90 billion = $67.50
4. NATO share on US Debt***
     25% x $79 Billion   = $19.75
5. Veterans served in NATO
     25% x $34 Billion= $ 8.50
6. Military Aid 1/7 x $7 Bil =   INC

TOTAL= $114.87 Billion

Table 5[41]

that the U.S. annual overseas Operations & Maintenance (O&M) budget is $90 billion[42] and 75 percent of major U.S. bases are in NATO countries as seen in Table 2, O&M for NATO bases costs the American taxpayer roughly $67.50 billion. If these costs are added to a conservative estimate, say 25 percent (instead of the 50 percent used in the Congressional formula) to allocate the portion of the U.S. defense budget attributed to both interest on U.S. debt and benefits for veterans having served in Europe (Table 3), then the annual cost of NATO exceeds $100 billion.

Breakout of Representative O&M Expenses

In 1988 the Americans spent billions of dollars to support NATO. Money was spent to repair and construct bases, to employ over 120,000 foreign nationals, for overseas cost-of-living differentials and supplements, for base operation costs, travel and permanent change of station costs and for financing currency fluctuations. Additionally, the Pentagon operated 271 schools in 19 countries for 155,000 American children and shipped almost 50,000 cars to Europe--the cost of shipping exceeding the value of the car in some cases.[43]

Supporting Germany is the most expensive U.S. cost of NATO. As of July 1990, Germany hosted over 200 major U.S. bases and 200,000 personnel costing the U.S. almost $11.8 billion. In addition, the U.S. flew about 12,000 US troops and 10,000 dependents between the U.S. and Germany on average for every month in 1988. Family travel for permanent change of station to Germany cost about $4,000 per enlisted and $13,000 per officer.[44] Furthermore, it costs the United States 10-20 percent more to maintain and operate forces overseas than in the United States.[45] Germany costs the U.S. a great deal of money.

Additional Consequences of NATO Costs

U.S. basing should have real purpose and add flexibility to American power projection. Since the strategic necessity for basing U.S. forces in Europe is gone, it is difficult to justify to the American people why more forces overseas are not cut and why the U.S. is still paying its 27 percent assessed share for the building of European bases absent a significant threat to European security.[46] It is also difficult to explain why foreign national employees paid by and working for the U.S. on bases in Europe are not being laid off even though the forces they are paid to support have been eliminated.[47] Some U.S. costs of NATO no longer make sense and should be stopped.

Congress is getting involved because many Americans are demanding a change to what overseas forces cost the U.S. "We are spending over $100 billion a year to pay the military bills for Europe and Japan when we cannot pay our own bills," Sen Kent Conrad D-N.D. said at a Senate Budget Committee Hearing.[48] "We are losing out in this exchange and our subsidy by U.S. taxpayers of the defense of Japan gives them more of their own gross national product to invest in their own country for their own purposes."[49] Clearly the rising cost of overseas basing is becoming an important issue to Congress in evaluating our forward deployed policy.

This issue is having an affect. The House voted in June 1992 to increase the cost to South Korea and NATO allies for U.S. forward deployed troops (vote 396 to 9), to reduce the FY 1993 defense bill by cutting funds for U.S. troops in Europe, Japan and South Korea (vote 220 to 185), and to reduce the number of U.S. troops in Europe from 235,700 to 100,000 by 1995 (241 to 162).[50] The National Defense Authorization Act for FY 1992 and 1993 H.R. 2100 Report of the Committee on Armed Services House of Representatives May 13, 1991--American Military Presence Abroad starts out by reporting:

> Nearly eighteen months ago the Berlin Wall fell, and with it the nightmare of a surprise Soviet bloc military attack on Western Europe. At the same time, host nation capabilities in Japan and Korea vastly improved--for reasons both military and budgetary, the US should reduce the number of troops it has stationed abroad.[51]

Overseas basing becomes more unpopular with each U.S. defense cut.

U.S. government and non-government organizations have made many Europeans aware of the changing attitude. The U.S. is taking a tougher stance in negotiating overseas basing rights as old agreements expire. As a result, new agreements more directly focus on reducing the cost to the U.S. while foreign countries ask for higher rent. Marc Fisher from the <u>Washington Post</u> Foreign Service reported that both Republicans and Democrats told European leaders that a new domestic focus among Americans is leading calls for a tougher stance on trade and for further troop reductions in Europe.[52] Speaking at the annual Munich Conference on Security policy, Sen William Cohen (R-Maine) said the "prevailing view" in the United States is that the North Atlantic Treaty Organization "is no longer necessary, relevant or affordable."[53] He said the alliance will likely become a "mainly European Organization,"[54] and that there was little support in Congress to maintain 150,000 U.S. troops in Europe.[55]

Even though each new Administration seeks to retain strong ties to Europe, saying they are essential to U.S. economic and security interests, the real heart of the matter is economics, not security. Melvyn Krauss, professor of economics at New York University, argues that the "economic recovery of allied nations has not uniformly been accompanied with any obligation on their part to join the U.S. in protecting the way of life and the values that we share."[56] He further says that "[w]hile American allies in NATO should do more for their own defense, another element must be the responsibility of others, like Japan and Germany," as friends, allies and world powers, to assume a greater responsibility for world crises.[57]

Numerous examples exist of the growing capacity of our allies to pay the bill. In FY 1992, while the Germans were paying roughly one quarter for our German basing costs, they announced that they would be willing to spend $8 billion over five years to house Russian troops leaving the former East Germany. That is the same amount Germany paid the U.S. over the last five years to protect its security.[58] Clearly, the Germans could have done more for the U.S. if they wanted to. Germany only pays 18% of the salaries the U.S. government pays to foreign nationals who work on U.S. bases in Germany.[59]

The U.S. is required to pay severance under German law to German workers who will lose their jobs as a result of the military drawdown.[60] Korea pays 11% more to the

U.S. for its foreign nationals than Germany.[61] "In 1991, the U.S. spent $1,180 per capita for defense of the world and Germany spent $446 per capita."[62] Japan pays for almost all U.S. military construction costs in the country and will assume labor and utility costs under a new agreement.[63] But Japan still ranks lower than all NATO countries in its share of gross domestic product devoted to defense.[64]

Some argue that the economic cost of disengagement is prohibitive given present American domestic concerns. Former Bush Administration officials argue that the cost of demobilization and withdrawal is high. Disengagement requires an immediate cost be paid to receive the larger and longer-term benefit associated with it. If the full cost of disengagement can not be afforded now, fewer bases can be closed until the longer-term economic benefits begin to accrue. When the U.S. economy improves and the work force becomes more stable, more overseas bases can be closed.

The top economic countries in the world probably benefit most from a stable world order. Countries like Germany and Japan thus ought to share more of the cost and burden of maintaining stability in the world. The new world order should be based on a strong network of allies, not weak alliances that foster permanent dependency. Weak alliances tend to rely first upon the U.S. as the sole policemen of the world and not upon their own strengths.[65]

Notes

32."The U.S. as the World's Policeman? Ten Reasons to Find a Different Role," The Defense Monitor, XX, No. 1, (1991), p. 1-2.
"Defending America: CDI Options for Military Spending," The Defense Monitor, XXI, No. 4, (1992), p.4.

33.This figure is derived from a Department of Defense annual report to Congress on the cost of the U.S. commitments to NATO. Memorandum, Ronald E. Porten, Force and Infrastructure, Cost Analysis Division, Office of the Assistant Secretary of Defense, to David Chu, Assistant Secretary of Defense, Program Analysis and Evaluation, through Dave McNicol and John Morgan, subject: ASD(LA) Question Related to the Cost of U.S. Forces for NATO Report, June 29, 1992, p. Tab A.

34.Ibid.

Notes

35."The U.S. as the World's Policeman? Ten Reasons to Find A Different Role," The Defense Monitor, XX, No. 1, (1991), p. 4.

36. Government military spending figures do not tell the whole story. The official "National Defense" category excludes several important military related expenses. When they are included, military spending comes to about $416, rather than $291 Billion [FY 1993] Sources: CDI, DOD, CEP.
"Defending America: CDI Options for Military Spending," The Defense Monitor, XXI, No. 4, (1992), p. 2.

37.Memorandum, Ronald E. Porten, Force and Infrastructure, Cost Analysis Division, Office of the Assistant Secretary of Defense, to David Chu, Assistant Secretary of Defense, Program Analysis and Evaluation, through Dave McNicol and John Morgan, subject: ASD(LA) Question Related to the Cost of U.S. Forces for NATO Report, June 29, 1992, p. Tab A.
Hearing Before the Committee on the Budget, House of Representatives, 102nd Cong., 2nd sess., ser. 102-32, Feb 5, 1992. (Washington: U.S. Government Printing Office, 1992), p. 156.

38.Memorandum, Ronald E. Porten, Force and Infrastructure, Cost Analysis Division, Office of the Assistant Secretary of Defense, to David Chu, Assistant Secretary of Defense, Program Analysis and Evaluation, through Dave McNicol and John Morgan, subject: ASD(LA) Question Related to the Cost of U.S. Forces for NATO Report, June 29, 1992, p. Tab A.

39.Hearing Before the Committee on the Budget, House of Representatives, 102nd Cong., 2nd sess., ser. 102-32, Feb 5, 1992. (Washington: U.S. Government Printing Office, 1992), p. 160.

40.Information Paper from The Office of the Chief of Staff, U.S. Army, subject: Cost Comparison, Mar. 11, 1992, p. 1.

41.Information Paper from Office of the Chief of Staff of the Army compared average cost/soldier for conus versus overseas assignments Europe. Cost comparison is based upon a generic mechanized division with identical TOE, fully manned and equipped, maintained at equal levels of readiness, operated at programmed OPTEMPO, and includes marginal base operations and real property maintenance. Memo concludes that cost for basing is 10-20 percent higher overseas.
Assumptions for above calculation:
** Army units comprise majority of personnel stationed in Europe and Air Force personnel and equipment (aircraft, spares, Pol) are at least as expensive as average cost of maintaining an army mechanized division.
*** Some portion of interest on US debt and US cost of veterans is due to our forward deployment policy. 25 percent was picked as a conservative estimate.
Information Paper from The Office of the Chief of Staff, U.S. Army, subject: Cost Comparison, Mar. 11, 1992, p. 1.

42."The Global Network of United States Military Bases," The Defense Monitor, XVIII, No. 2, (1989), p. 2.

43.Hearings Before House Armed Services Committee, Subcommittee on Readiness, subject: Cost of Operating Overseas Bases, Statement of W. Bruce Weinrod, Deputy Assistant Secretary of Defense (European and NATO Policy), April 3, 1990, p. 1.

Notes

"The U.S. as the World's Policeman? Ten Reasons to Find a Different Role," The Defense Monitor, XX, No. 1, (1991), p. 7.

44.Ibid.

45.Information Paper from The Office of the Chief of Staff, U.S. Army, subject: Cost Comparison, Mar. 11, 1992, p. 1.

46.Ambassador H. Allen Holmes, personal interview in Washington D.C., Dec. 1992.
John Thompson, "NATO Program Proves Vital," Defense News, (Dec. 7-13, 1992), p. 28.
Philip Finnegan and Theresa Hitchens, "U.S. Cut of NATO Funds May Spur Allied Rebuff," Defense News, (Oct. 12, 1992), p. 4.

47.Hearings Before House Armed Services Committee, Subcommittee on Readiness, subject: Cost of Operating Overseas Bases, Statement of Congressman Paul E. Kanjorski, April 3, 1990, p. 1.

48.Philip Finnegan, "Allies' Burden-Sharing Issue Rankles Congress," Defense News, (Feb. 10, 1992), p. 8.

49.Ibid.

50."House Votes to Cut Overseas Forces," The Washington Post, (June 4, 1992), p. A5.

51.H.R.Report 2100, National Defense Authorization Act for Fiscal Years 1992 and 1993, Report of the Committee on Armed Services, 102d Cong., 1st sess., 1991, p. 289.

52.Marc Fisher, "Europeans Told of U.S. Isolationism: Congressmen Signal Slipping Commitment To Atlantic Alliance," Washington Post, (Feb. 2, 1992), p. 1.

53.Ibid.

54.Ibid.

55.Patrick E. Tyler, "U.S. Army Gets Flexibility on Europe Troop Levels," The New York Times International, (June 18, 1992), p. A15.
Hearings Before House Armed Services Committee, Subcommittee on Readiness, subject: Cost of Operating Overseas Bases, Opening Statement by Chairman Earl Hutto, April 3, 1990, p. 2.

56.Melvyn Krauss, a senior fellow at the Hoover Institution on War, Revolution, and Peace and Professor of economics at New York University, "Seven Myths About NATO", Imprimis, (Oct. 1988), p. 2.

57.Ibid.

58.Frank Lautenberg, "U.S. Must Spread Expense of Overseas Basing to Wealthy Allies." Remarks are excerpted from Aug. 12, 1992 speech supporting an amendment to the appropriations bill. Published Aug. 31, 1992.

59.Ibid.

Notes

60. Ibid.

61. Ibid.

62. Ibid.

63. Ibid.

64. Defense Expenditures of NATO Countries 1970-1990.   Table compiled by NATO's Statistical Analysis Service.
Philip Finnegan, "Allies' Burden-Sharing Issue Rankles Congress," Defense News, (Feb. 10, 1992), p. 8.
"U. S. and NATO: Press Background," Center for Defense Information Press Release, (Feb 24, 1988), p. 1.

65. "The U. S. as the World's Policeman?   Ten Reasons to Find a Different Role," The Defense Monitor, XX, No. 1, (1991), p. 4.

V. Is Now The Right Time To Pull Back?

Now is the right time for the United States to withdraw most of the U.S. military forces forward deployed in Europe. Our forces should not be made less flexible and unable to respond to world crises because they are permanently deployed in Europe. While forward bases may continue to be convenient, they are not vital, and are expensive.[66]

U.S. military forces not forward deployed have the ability to respond quickly to crises anywhere in the world, which allows us to respond to any European threat to our national interest that we can foresee today. American inflight refueling, new strategic weapons, stealth, strategic satellites, and over-the-horizon communications give us a technological edge today not available fifty years ago.[67] For example, the U.S. airlifted more personnel and equipment in the first three weeks of Desert Storm than it moved during the first three months of Korea. By the 6th week the U.S. already had moved the air equivalent of what was delivered during the entire 65 weeks of the 1948-49 Berlin Airlift.[68] This mobility would allow the U.S. to respond to a threat in Europe. Additionally there is no legal or treaty requirement to have U.S. troops and weapons in place in foreign countries.[69]

Europeans have more potential to defend themselves today then in the previous fifty years. They now provide 90% of land forces, 75% of naval forces and 50% of air forces for NATO defense.[70] In short, U.S. participation in NATO may not be needed, but it is expensive.

Furthermore, our military forces in NATO do not assure economic access and political influence. Some argue that it is in the interest of the U.S. to keep military forces abroad because their presence in foreign countries enhances America's "status," guarantees the U.S. a voice in the affairs of the host countries, and reassures American companies conducting overseas business.[71] This concept is increasingly outdated in a world where the economic instrument of national power is seemingly becoming dominant. Total two-way American trade with Europe exceeds $200 billion annually; with East Asia the figure is higher--$300 billion. Having U.S. military forces present however may contribute little in most cases to America's economic access and political influence around the world. On the contrary, it may actually weaken U.S. security by placing unnecessary strains on its economy by relieving our major economic competitors, Germany and Japan, of providing for their own defense.[72] The U.S. still has the largest economy in the world. By virtue of this fact, it will have access, troops or no troops.[73] There is little recent evidence that having U.S. forces in Europe translates into political influence. It is in the interest of the U.S. to remain actively engaged in the world's affairs, but primarily through economic and diplomatic efforts which are much less reliant on the military instrument of power.[74]

Our allies complicated the situation by developing strong economies and becoming effective trade competitors with the U.S. Japan supplanted or is replacing the U.S. as the world's leading producer of TVs, VCRs, computer chips, automobiles, mainframe computers, etc. West Germany has become the biggest economy in Europe and the world's premier exporter. The U.S. maintains an unequal burden by expending economic resources on the defense of allies who spend their resources on their own economic infrastructure instead. This could place the U.S. at an economic disadvantage.

Unfortunately, many of our leaders declined to keep up with the rapid changes of the new world situation by solving the associated economic problems. General John Galvin, former NATO military commander, argued for old policies: "[b]y 1995, our European based forces will number around 150,000, a reduction of more than fifty percent. Thus the "Base Force" will consist of a two division corps, more than three tactical fighter wing equivalents, the Sixth fleet with a carrier battle group and a Marine amphibious unit, along with the intelligence, communications, and reception infrastructure required to expedite return of U.S. forces to Europe should the need arise."[75] When asked what threat justifies this force, General Galvin said, "When you have the question of insecurity and instability and unpredictability, then what you need is structure, and NATO is the best structure, the best military-political structure, I think the world has ever seen in history."[76] NATO is seen by Army generals as necessary, because the Army can not get its equipment to the battle in under 30 days if it is not already prepositioned.

Our present expenditures for NATO are becoming more difficult to justify while the support of our allies may not be as dependable as we would like. Although the Europeans did share the risks and costs in the Gulf War, they did come late to the conflict. The United States faces twin budget and trade deficits which makes it increasingly difficult for us to afford forward deployment in Europe. There is an ever-widening national consensus that our military spending must be held down. Our present lack of economic competitiveness in the world today instills a sense of urgency in any burden sharing debate. A large proportion of the United States defense budget is devoted to the defense of allies, guaranteeing that the first battle of the next war would be fought of foreign soil. But in the final analysis many countries, including our allies, receive benefits from U.S. peace-maintaining operations without each sharing the burden according to its own means.

Notes

66.Ibid., p. 5.

67.Ibid.

68."The U.S. as the World's Policeman? Ten Reasons to Find a Different Role," The Defense Monitor, XX, No. 1, (1991), p. 5.

69.Ibid., p. 3,5.

70."NATO: Is It Time to Withdraw?" CATO Policy Report, p. 6.
Frank J. Richter, "Do NATO Allies Contribute Their Fair Share?" Detroit News, (Mar. 31, 1989), p. 18.

71.Ibid.

Notes

72.Ibid.

73.Ibid., p. 6.

74.Ibid.

75.Statement of General John R. Galvin, Commander in Chief, United States European Command before the United States Senate Committee on Foreign Relations, (July 25, 1991), p. 6.
John Lancaster, "Top General Supports 150,000 U. S. Troops in Europe as Hedge," The Washington Post, (Mar. 4, 1992), p. A20.
Patrick E. Tyler, "U.S. Army Gets Flexibility on Europe Troop Levels," The New York Times International, (June 18, 1992), p. A15.
Andrew Borowiec, "Kohl to Press Here for U. S. Presence in Europe," The Washington Times, (March 20, 1992), p. A7.

76.Statement of General John R. Galvin, Commander in Chief, United States European Command before the United States Senate Committee on Foreign Relations, (July 25, 1991), p. 6.

VI. Options

The U.S. should investigate several options that lie between the status quo and complete withdrawal. Keeping in mind that the object is to maximize security and flexibility at the best cost, these options allow the U.S. to stay involved in Europe while recognizing the new reality of post-Cold War Europe.

OPTION 1

Allow NATO to keep its new peacekeeping mission, withdraw U.S. military from European countries and replace U.S. presence in Europe with a Rapid Deployment Force (RDF). The RDF could be formed by leaving three fighter squadron equivalents in the United Kingdom and stationing a total of 2-3000 U.S. Army and Marines in Italy. The units should possess enough airlift and prepositioned assets to be rapidly deployable in six hours to any location in Western Europe and the Mediterranean. The U.S. should relinquish leadership responsibilities for NATO, but remain as a member offering its RDF and accompanied airlift as potential elements for NATO's peacekeeping mission. Having U.S. forces stationed in Europe should provide the legitimacy required for U.S. continued membership in NATO, which has become more of a political organization than a peacemaking force. Other U.S forces previously stationed in NATO countries providing unique capabilities, not directly related to the NATO peacekeeping mission like air refueling or ground station support for U.S. satellites, should remain.

Units removed from NATO should be reestablished in higher threat areas or brought home. A second RDF, sized according to the potential threats in Asia, should be positioned in Japan. This would give the U.S. a quick response to crises in Asia until other assets from the U.S. could respond.

The U.S. leadership structure, command and control infrastructure, and essential personnel to maintain stored U.S. equipment in NATO should remain. This is in addition to other U.S. forces deployed in Europe for other than NATO missions. Deploy and exercise U.S. forces from the CONUS to Europe once every three years to operate the equipment. This will allow the United States military to identify its deficiencies.

A secondary benefit of this option is that unilateral U.S. withdrawal from NATO should result in establishing another European forum to provide regional security. Any such group, like the Western European Union (WEU), should include a predictable rotating leadership from Germany, France and United Kingdom. A rotating leadership could act to prevent a future French, German or British hegemon from consolidating its leadership position in Europe. However, this should remain a European decision while the U.S. seeks its own national interest.

Final Note

European countries are searching for their own identity, leadership, and direction. By maintaining the status quo, U.S. domestic and foreign trade pressures will continue to generate dissent by our Allies in European affairs. It is not a coincidence that Europe continues to form new organizations without U.S. membership to deal with European economic, political, and security needs.

There are no significant economic reasons for the U.S. to remain in NATO. NATO is expensive, the threat to Europe has disappeared, and Europeans have the potential to provide for their own security.

A reduced threat offers a rare opportunity to reevaluate our forward deployment policy. The 100 billion dollars spent on Europe could be more effectively spent to create and maintain a rapidly deployed and flexible force in the United States. This force could respond more quickly to crises in remote corners of the world and save billions of dollars in the process. Unfortunately, troops deployed in Europe will be of little value in potential trouble spots in Asia and the Caribbean, especially if they train only for a European scenario. This reality demands that American policy makers reexamine our security commitments on a global basis rather than a regional one. This is merely a recognition of the need to know when to change or terminate a security arrangement once it out-lives its effectiveness. The reliable and predictable environment of the Cold War has passed and we must seize this moment to set a new pattern for defense requirements. This new pattern will demand frequent review and a willingness to approach defense issues with a new attitude. President Clinton has the authority to eliminate all foreign bases not deemed essential to U.S. security. He should begin that process in Europe.

APPENDIX 1

The North Atlantic Treaty
Washington D.C., 4 April 1949

The Parties to this Treaty reaffirm their faith in the purposes and principles of the Charter of the United Nations and their desire to live in peace with all peoples and all governments.
They are determined to safeguard the freedom, common heritage and civilization of their peoples, founded on the principles of democracy, individual liberty and the rule of law.
They seek to promote stability and well-being in the North Atlantic area.
They are resolved to unite their efforts for collective defence and for the preservation of peace and security.
They therefore agree to this North Atlantic Treaty:

ARTICLE 1
The Parties undertake, as set forth in the Charter of the United Nations, to settle any international dispute in which they may be involved by peaceful means in such a manner that international peace and security and justice are not endangered, and to refrain in their international relations from the threat or use of force in any manner inconsistent with the purposes of the United Nations.

ARTICLE 2
The Parties will contribute toward the further development of peaceful and friendly international relations by strengthening their free institutions, by bringing about a better understanding of the principles upon which these institutions are founded, and by promoting conditions of stability and well-being. They will seek to eliminate conflict in their international economic policies and will encourage economic collaboration between any or all of them.

ARTICLE 3
In order more effectively to achieve the objectives of this Treaty, the Parties, separately and jointly, by means of continuous and effective self-help and mutual aid, will maintain and develop their individual and collective capacity to resist armed attack.

ARTICLE 4
The Parties will consult together whenever, in the opinion of any of them, the territorial integrity, political independence or security of any of the Parties is threatened.

ARTICLE 5
The Parties agree that an armed attack against one or more of them in Europe or North America shall be considered an attack against them all and consequently they agree that, if such an armed attack occurs, each of them, in exercise of the right of individual or

collective self-defence recognized by Article 51 of the Charter of the United Nations, will assist the Party or Parties so attacked by taking forthwith, individually and in concert with the other Parties, such action as it deems necessary, including the use of armed force, to restore and maintain the security of the North Atlantic area.

Any such armed attack and all measures taken as a result thereof shall immediately be reported to the Security Council. Such measures shall be terminated when the Security Council has taken the measures necessary to restore and maintain international peace and security.

ARTICLE 6

For the purpose of Article V an armed attack on one or more of the Parties is deemed to include an armed attack on the territory of any of the Parties in Europe or North America, on the Algerian Departments of France, on the occupation forces of any Party in Europe, on the islands under the jurisdiction of an Party in the North Atlantic area north of the Tropic of Cancer or on the vessels or aircraft in this area of any of the Parties.

ARTICLE 7

This Treaty does not affect, and shall not be interpreted as affecting, in any way the rights and obligations under the Charter of the Parties which are members of the United Nations, or the primary responsibility of the Security Council for the maintenance of international peace and security.

ARTICLE 8

Each Party declares that none of the international engagements now in force between it and any other of the Parties or any third State is in conflict with the provisions of this Treaty, and undertakes not to enter into any international engagement in conflict with this Treaty.

ARTICLE 9

The Parties hereby establish a Council, on which each of them shall be represented, to consider matters concerning the implementation of this Treaty. The Council shall be so organized as to be able to meet promptly at any time. The Council shall set up such subsidiary bodies as may be necessary; in particular it shall establish immediately a defence committee which shall recommend measures for the implementation of Articles III and V.

ARTICLE 10

The Parties may, by unanimous agreement, invite any other European State in a position to further the principles of this Treaty and to contribute to the security of the North Atlantic area to accede to this Treaty. Any State so invited may become a Party to the Treaty by depositing its instrument of accession with the Government of the United States of America. The Government of the United States of America will inform each of the Parties of the deposit of each such instrument of accession.

ARTICLE 11

This Treaty shall be ratified and its provisions carried out by the Parties in accordance with their respective constitutional processes. The instruments of ratification shall be deposited as soon as possible with the Government of the United States of America, which will notify all the other signatories of each deposit. The Treaty shall enter into force between the States which have ratified it as soon as the ratifications of the majority of the signatories, including the ratification of Belgium, Canada, France, Luxembourg, the Netherlands, the United Kingdom and the United States, have been deposited and shall come into effect with respect to other States on the date of the deposit of their ratifications.

ARTICLE 12

After the Treaty has been in force for ten years, or at any time thereafter, the Parties shall, if any of them so requests, consult together for the purpose of reviewing the Treaty, having regard for the factors then affecting peace and security in the North Atlantic area, including the development of universal as well as regional arrangements under the Charter of the United Nations for the maintenance of international peace and security.

ARTICLE 13

After the Treaty has been in force for twenty years, any Party may cease to be a Party one year after its notice of denunciation has been given to the Government of the United States of America, which will inform the Governments of the other Parties of the deposit of each notice of denunciation.

ARTICLE 14

This Treaty, of which the English and French texts are equally authentic, shall be deposited in the archives of the Government of the United States of America. Duly certified copies will be transmitted by that Government to the governments of the other signatories.

BIBLIOGRAPHY

PRIMARY SOURCES

Acheson, Dean. "Peace and Security for North Atlantic Nations." <u>Vital Speeches of the Day</u>, April 15, 1949, p. 386-391.

_____. "Practical Effects of Proposed Military Assistance." <u>The Department of State Bulletin</u>, Aug. 22, 1949, p. 264-269.

_____. <u>Present At The Creation: My Years in the State Department.</u> New York: W. W. Norton & Company, 1969.

_____. "Problems in American Foreign Policy." <u>The Department of State Bulletin</u>, Oct. 31, 1949, p. 668-671.

_____. "Purpose of Proposed North Atlantic Treaty." <u>The Department of State Bulletin</u>, Jan 30, 1949, p. 160.

_____. "Request for Military Assistance From Atlantic Pact Countries." <u>The Department of State Bulletin</u>, April 17, 1949, p. 493-498.

_____. "Senate Approves Ratification of North Atlantic Treaty." <u>The Department of State Bulletin</u>, Aug. 1, 1949, p. 148.

_____. "The Atlantic Pact." <u>Vital Speeches of the Day</u>, April 1, 1949, p. 355-358.

_____. "The Meaning of the North Atlantic Pact." <u>The Department of State Bulletin</u>, Washington D.C.: U.S. Government Printing Office, March 27, 1949, p. 384-388.

_____. "The North Atlantic Treaty and the Role of the Military Assistance Program." <u>The Department of State Bulletin</u>, May 8, 1949, p. 594-599.

_____. "The Preservation of Peace." <u>Vital Speeches of the Day</u>, Feb. 15, 1949, p. 259-260.

"Administration and Cost of ERP Hotly Debated By Congress." <u>Foreign Policy Bulletin</u>, Jan. 16, 1948, p.8.

Aldrich, Winthrop W. "American Interest in European Reconstruction." An address before the 73rd Annual Convention American Bankers Association, Atlantic City, NJ. Sep 30, 1947.

Austin, Warren R. "A More Perfect Union." <u>The Department of State Bulletin</u>, Jan 27, 1949, p. 278-281.

_____. "Formula for World Peace." <u>Vital Speeches of the Day</u>, Nov. 15, 1946, p. 80-85.

_____. "The Proposed North Atlantic Pact." The <u>Department of State Bulletin</u>, March 6, 1949, p. 298-300.

_____. "U.S. Answers Soviet Charges Against North Atlantic Treaty." <u>The Department of State Bulletin</u>, April 24, 1949, p. 552-555.

_____. "Why We Support the U.N." The <u>Department of State Bulletin</u>, Oct 31, 1948, p. 551-554.

_____. "World Confidence and the Reduction of Armed Forces: The American Objective." <u>The Department of State Bulletin</u>, Oct. 24, 1948, p. 511-514.

Bechhoefer, Bernhard G. "Voting in the Security Council." <u>The Department of State Bulletin</u>, July 4, 1948, p. 3-8.

Beckett, Sir W. Eric. <u>The North Atlantic Treaty, The Brussels Treaty, and The Charter of the United Nations</u>. London: Stevens & Sons Limited, 1950.

Bevin, Ernest. "The Organization of the Post-War World." <u>Vital Speeches of the Day</u>, Feb. 1, 1948, p. 226-234.

_____. "United Nations' Problems." <u>Vital Speeches of the Day</u>, Oct. 15, 1948, p. 2-7.

Bohlen, Charles E. "American Aid in Restoring the European Community." <u>The Department of State Bulletin</u>, Jan. 18, 1948, p. 78-82.

_____. "The North Atlantic Pact: A Historic Step in the Development of American Foreign Relations." <u>The Department of State Bulletin</u>, April 3, 1949, p. 428-429.

Bolles, Blair. "North Atlantic Defense Pact Background." <u>Foreign Policy Reports</u>, Feb. 15, 1949, p. 226-228.

Britain and U.S. Face Need For Mutual Adjustments." <u>Foreign Policy Bulletin</u>, Sep. 2, 1949.

Britain's Crisis Tests U.S. Economic Policy." <u>Foreign Policy Bulletin</u>, July 29, 1949.

Brown, Winthrop G. "Economic Factors in U.S. Foreign Policy." <u>The Department of State Bulletin</u>, Aug. 15, 1948, p. 203-207.

Byrnes, James F. "America's Position on World Problems: We Must Live by the Charter." <u>Vital Speeches of the Day</u>, March 15, 1946, p. 326-329.

_____. "Common Interests Far Outweigh Conflicting Interests: Nations Cannot Live with Themselves Alone." Vital Speeches of the Day, Feb. 1, 1946, p. 240-241.

_____. "Creating Real World Peace." Vital Speeches of the Day, Feb. 1, 1947, p. 231-233.

Cable News Network. Interview with Gen. Colin Powell, Nov. 25, 1991.

Caine, Steven A., Col. USAF. Department of State, Washington D. C., Personal Interview, 16 Dec 1992.

Calhoun, Martin L. Center for Defense Information, Washington D. C., Personal Interview, 16 Dec 1992.

Cardozo, Michael H. "Foreign Aid Articles and the Burden of Loss." The Department of State Bulletin, Aug. 15, 1949, p. 215-228.

Carey, Jane Perry Clark. "Western European Union and the Atlantic Community." Foreign Policy Reports, June 15, 1950, p. 66-79.

"Ceremony of the North Atlantic Treaty, Departmental Auditorium, April 4, 1949." The Department of State Bulletin, April 17, 1949, p. 471-482.

Cheney, Dick. "U.S. Forward Presence In Asia and NATO." Defense Issues, Vol. 5, No. 20, April 24, 1990, p. 1-4.

Churchill, Winston. "Alliance of English-Speaking People." Vital Speeches of the Day, March 15, 1946, p. 329-332.

_____. "Peace Rests Upon Strength." Vital Speeches of the Day, Nov. 1, 1948, p. 44-45.

"Conflicting Administration Views Impede U.S. Policy." Foreign Policy Bulletin, June 2, 1950.

"Congress Weighs Implementation of Atlantic Pact." Foreign Policy Bulletin, July 15, 1949.

"Congressional Leaders Reappraise ERP." Foreign Policy Bulletin, Dec. 17, 1948.

Congressional Record. 80th Cong., 2nd Sess., Vol. 94-Part 2, Feb 20 to March 15, 1948.

Congressional Record. 80th Cong., 2nd Sess., Vol. 94-Part 3, March 16 - April 8, 1948.

Congressional Record. 80th Cong., 2nd Sess., Vol. 94-Part 5, May 12, 1948-June 2,

1948.

Congressional Record. 80th Cong., 2nd Sess., Vol. 94-Part 6, June 3- June 14, 1948.

Congressional Record. 81st Cong., 1st Sess., Vol. 95-Part 3, Mar 21 to April 2, 1949.

Congressional Record. 81st Cong., 1st Sess., Vol. 95-Part 5, May 5 to May 21, 1949.

Congressional Record. 81st Cong., 1st Sess., Vol. 95-Part 7, June 28 to July 20, 1949.

Congressional Record. 81st Cong., 1st Sess., Vol. 95-Part 8, July 21 to Aug 11, 1949.

Connally, Tom. "Senate Debate on the North Atlantic Treaty." The Department of State Bulletin, July 18, 1949, p. 53-68.

Cost Comparison: Information Paper from the Office of the Chief of Staff, U.S. Army. Mar. 11, 1992, p. 1.

Dean, Vera Micheles. "Pros and Cons of North Atlantic Defense Pact." Foreign Policy Reports, Feb. 15, 1949, p. 228-232.

_____. "Should the U. S. Re-examine Its Foreign Policy?" Foreign Policy Reports, Dec. 15, 1949, p. 178-191.

Dean, Vera Micheles and Gray, Howard C. "Military and Economic Strength of Western Europe." Foreign Policy Reports, Oct. 15, 1950, p. 118-123.

Department of State. Germany 1947-1949: The Story in Documents. Washington, D. C.: US Gov't Printing Office, 1950.

"Differing Aims Test Unity of Atlantic Powers." Foreign Policy Bulletin, April 8, 1949.

Douglas, Louis and Grady, Henry F. "Testimony on Military Assistance Programs." The Department of State Bulletin, Aug. 15, 1949, p. 229-235.

"Economic Cooperation Act of 1948." The Department of State Bulletin, May 16, 1948, p. 640-641.

Eisenhower, Dwight D. "Support for Western Europe: Political as Well as Economic Unity." Vital Speeches of the Day, May 15, 1948, p. 461-463.

"ERP Agreements Concluded With Fourteen Countries." The Department of State Bulletin, July 25, 1948, p. 104.

"ERP Gives U.S. New Lever In East-West Struggle." Foreign Policy Bulletin, April 16, 1948.

"Europe's Poverty Challenges All Ideologies." Foreign Policy Bulletin, Nov. 11, 1949.

"Fact Sheet, Department of Defense, Worldwide Military Strength as of June 30, 1992." News Release, Office of Assistant Secretary of Defense, Washington, D.C. Oct 20, 1992.

"France Aspires To Western Union Leadership." Foreign Policy Bulletin, Mar. 25, 1949.

Galvin, Gen John R. Committee on Foreign Relations, U.S. Senate. Statement, July 25, 1991.

Gross, Ernest A. "Foreign Aid and Reconstruction: International Law and the European Recovery Program." The Department of State Bulletin, May 2, 1948, p. 564-567.

_____. "The European recovery Program Agreements - A New International Era." The Department of State Bulletin, July 4, 1948, p. 35-42.

Hale, Robert F. Committee on Armed Services, House of Representatives. Statement before the Defense Burdensharing Panel, May 10, 1988.

Harris, Seymour E. "ERP: Progress and Prospects." Foreign Policy Reports, April 15, 1949, p. 30-39.

Harris, Seymour E. and Harris, Ruth B. "ECA and Intra-European Trade." Foreign Policy Reports, April 15, 1949, p. 40.

Hart, Merwin K. "Political Implication of the Marshall Plan: Socialist Western European Union." Vital Speeches of the Day, Feb. 15, 1948, p. 278-282.

Holmes, H. Allen. Ambassador, Personal Interview. Washington, D. C., 16 Dec 1992.

Hutcheson, Harold H. "European Recovery Program: Problems and Prospects." Foreign Policy Reports, Dec. 15, 1947, pp. 238-247.

Hutcheson, Harold H. and Ringwood, Ona K.D. "The Impact of Foreign Aid on U. S. Economy." Foreign Policy Reports, Dec. 15, 1947.

Jessup, Philip C. "International Security Through the United Nations and the Atlantic Pact." Department of State Bulletin, Washington D.C.: U.S. Government Printing Office, 1949.

Johnston, Eric. "Partners for Peace: American Production Loans to Private European Enterprises." Vital Speeches of the Day, Mar. 15, 1948, p. 329-331.

Kanjorski, Paul E. Committee on Armed Services Subcommittee on Readiness. Statement. April 3, 1990.

"Letter From the American Ambassador to Great Britain to the Chairman of the Senate Foreign Relations Committee." The Department of State Bulletin, Feb. 22, 1948, p. 233-237.

Marshall, George C. "Assistance to European Economic Recovery." The Department of State Bulletin, Jan. 18, 1948, p. 71-77.

_____. "Firm and Determined Course for the Democracies." The Department of State Bulletin, May 30, 1948, p. 744-746.

_____. "No Compromise on Essential Freedoms." U.S. Dept of State, 1948.

_____. "Our Dominant Position of Leadership: Timely Action Required." Vital Speeches of the Day, April 1, 1948, p. 357-359.

_____. "Relation of European Recovery Program to American Foreign Policy." The Department of State Bulletin, Jan. 25, 1948, p. 112-114.

_____. "Relation of Military Strength to Diplomatic Action." The Department of State Bulletin, March 28, 1948, pp. 421.

_____. "Statement by Secretary Marshall Concerning Signing of Economic Cooperation Agreements." The Department of State Bulletin, July 4, 1948, p. 43.

_____. "Survival of Democracy Dependent on Success of ERP." The Department of State Bulletin, Feb. 22, 1948, p. 231-232.

_____. "The European Recovery Program: Full Aid or None." Vital Speeches of the Day, Jan. 15, 1948, p. 207-211.

_____. "The Third Regular Session of the General Assembly, Paris: No Compromise of Essential Freedoms." The Department of State Bulletin, Oct. 3, 1948, p. 432-435.

_____. "The Stake of the Businessman in the European Recovery Program." The Department of State Bulletin, Jan. 25, 1948, p. 108-111.

_____. "World-Wide Struggle Between Freedom and Tyranny." The Department of State Bulletin, March 28, 1948, p. 422-425.

"Military Aid Program Threatens to Overshadow ERP." Foreign Policy Bulletin, Dec. 30, 1949.

"Military Factors Play Major Part In Atlantic Pact." Foreign Policy Bulletin, Feb. 25, 1949.

"Mutual Aid Under ERP Gains Momentum." Foreign Policy Bulletin, Nov. 5, 1948.

"Mutual Defense Assistance Act of 1949." The Department of State Bulletin, Oct. 24, 1949, p. 603-608.

NATO Facts and Figures. Brussels: NATO Information Service, 1971.

NATO: Facts About the North Atlantic Treaty Organization. Netherlands: Bosch-Utrecht, 1962.

"NATO: Its Development and Significance." Department of State, 1957.

"NATO: The View from Europe." (Public Opinion) Current News Supplement, June 21, 1989, p. B20-B28.

Nitze, Paul H. "Sound International Trade Program: Its Meaning for American Business." The Department of State Bulletin, Nov. 7, 1948, p. 578-582.

"North Atlantic Treaty: Proposed for Signature During First Week in April, 1949." Department of State Bulletin, March 20, 1949, p. 339-342.

"Operation Provide Hope." Briefing on JFACC Operations to SAAS by Major Jim Brooks May 1993.

Peurifoy, Assistant Secretary. "Foreign Policy and the North Atlantic Pact." The Department of State Bulletin, May 15, 1949, p. 633-635.

Pocalyko, Michael N., Cmdr. US Navy. The Atlantic Council of the United States, Washington, D.C., Personal Interview, 17 Dec 1992.

Porten, Ronald E. "ASD(LA) Question Related to the Cost of U.S. Forces for NATO Report", Memorandum, Office of the Assistant Secretary of Defense, Washington D.C., June 29, 1992.

"Report of The Committee of Three on Non-Military Co-Operation in NATO." A report by the NATO Information Division, Paris, 1956.

"Report of the Secretary of State to the President on North Atlantic Treaty." The Department of State Bulletin, April 24, 1949, p. 532-536.

Shaud, John A. "NATO 1988 - 1991: A View Through Three Lenses." Air University Document, Feb. 1992.

Stassen, Harold E. "Marshall Plan, Europe's Only Alternative to Communism." Vital Speeches of the Day, Oct 15, 1947, p. 20-23.

Taft, Robert and Dulles, John F. "The North Atlantic Pact." Vital Speeches of the Day, Aug. 1, 1949, p. 610-623.

"The North Atlantic Pact: Collective Defense and the Preservation of Peace, Security, and Freedom in the North Atlantic Community." Department of State Bulletin, March 20, 1949, p. 342-350.

Thorp, Assistant Secretary. "Relationship of Economic Commission for Europe to European Recovery Program." The Department of State Bulletin, July 25, 1948, p. 118.

"Treaty of Economic, Social and Cultural Collaboration and Collective Self-Defence." The Department of State Bulletin, May 9, 1948, p. 600-602.

Truman, Harry S. "An Investment for Peace." Vital Speeches of the Day, Sept. 1, 1949, p. 674-676.

_____. "Essential Elements of Lasting Peace." The Department of State Bulletin, June 19, 1949, p. 771-773.

_____. "International Economic Policy." Vital Speeches of the Day, Sept. 1, 1949, p. 698-700.

_____. "President Truman Transmits the North Atlantic Treaty to the Senate." The Department of State Bulletin, May 8, 1949, p. 599-600.

_____. "Reciprocal Trade Agreements Extension Act Approved." The Department of State Bulletin, Oct. 10, 1949, p. 548-549.

_____. "Senate Approval of North Atlantic Pact." The Department of State Bulletin, Aug. 8, 1949, p. 199.

_____. "Signing of the Foreign Aid Appropriation Act." The Department of State Bulletin, July 4, 1948, p. 45-50.

_____. "The Coming Into Effect of the North Atlantic Treaty." The Department of State Bulletin, Sept. 5, 1949, p. 355.

_____. "Victory Without War." Vital Speeches of the Day, Aug. 1, 1949, p. 624-626.

Truman, Harry S. and Acheson, Dean. "Military Assistance Program Transmitted to the Congress." The Department of State Bulletin, Aug. 8, 1949, p. 186-199.

"U.S. Armed Forces in Europe: From burden Sharing to Burden Shedding." The Defense Monitor. Vol. XIX, Number 4. 1990, p. 1-7.

U.S Congress. House. Armed Services Committee. Cost of Operating Overseas Bases. Hearings before a Subcommittee on Readiness, April 3, 1990.

U.S. Congress. House. Committee on Armed Services. Defense Burdensharing: The Costs, Benefits, and Future of US Alliances. 100th Cong., 2nd Sess., Feb 2, Mar 1 and 2, 1988.

U.S. Congress. House. Committee on Armed Services. National Defense Authorization Act for Fiscal Years 1992 and 1993. H.R. Report 2100, 102d Cong., 1st Sess., 1991.

U.S. Congress. House. Committee on Foreign Affairs and its Subcommittee on Europe. U. S. Forces in NATO. 93rd Cong., June 18, 19, 25, 26; July 10,11,12, 17, 1973.

U.S. Congress. House. Committee on the Budget. 102 Cong., 2nd Sess., ser. 102-32, Feb 5, 1992.

U.S. Congress. House. Defense Burdensharing Panel of the Committee on Armed Services. Reaction to Burdensharing Proposals. 100th Cong., 2nd Sess., Sept. 27, 1988.

U.S. Congress. House. Defense Burdensharing Panel of the Committee on Armed Serves. The Balance of Military Forces.
100th Cong., 2nd Sess., March 3, 1988.

U.S. Congress. Senate. Committee on Foreign Relations. The Vandenberg Resolution and the North Atlantic Treaty. S. Res. 239, 80th Cong., 2nd Sess., and Executive L, 81st Cong., 1st Sess., 1973.

Vandenberg, Arthur H. "Our Mutual Problems with the World." Vital Speeches of the Day, Feb. 1, 1947, p. 228-231.

_____. "Soviet Pressure, a World Peril." Vital Speeches of the Day, April 15, 1947, p. 391-395.

_____. "The Economic Cooperation Administration: A Plan for Peace, Stability and Freedom." Vital Speeches of the Day, Mar. 15, 1948, p. 322-328.

_____. "What Is Russia Up To: Report on Un Meeting in London." Vital Speeches of the Day, March 15, 1946, p. 322-326.

Vandenberg, Arthur H. Jr. The Private Papers of Senator Vandenberg. Cambridge, MA: The Riverside Press, 1952.

"West European Unity No Panacea for Economic Ills." Foreign Policy Bulletin, Nov. 11, 1949.

"Western Europe Moves to Implement ERP Pledges." <u>Foreign Policy Bulletin</u>, April 9, 1948.

"Western Europe Unites to Check Communism." <u>Foreign Policy Bulletin</u>, March 19, 1948.

<u>SECONDARY SOURCES</u>

"Appendix F1-F80, Logistics Build Up and Sustainment". <u>Title V Report, Conduct of Persian Gulf War, Final Report to Congress</u>, April 1992.

Beatty, Jack. "The Exorbitant Anachronism." <u>The Atlantic Monthly</u>, June 1989, p. 40-51.

Betts, Richard K. "Systems for Peace or Causes of War? Collective Security, Arms Control, and the New Europe." <u>International Security</u>, Summer 1992, p. 5-43.

"Big Five' Weapons Exporters: More Talks, More Sales." <u>Arms Control Today</u>. Nov. 1991, p. 15.

Blackaby, Frank. "Burdensharing and Conventional Arms Control: The Next Steps in Europe." Washington, D.C.: The British American Security Information Council, no date.

Borowiec, Andrew. "Kohl to Press Here for U.S. Presence in Europe." <u>The Washington Times</u>, March 20, 1992.

Browers, Billy D. "Should the United States Remain in NATO and if so, How Should We Be Committed?" Unpublished master's thesis, Naval War College, Newport, RI, 1991.

"Burden Sharing An Overdue Final Chapter To WWII." A paper without an author or a date.

"Burdensharing" a paper without an author or a date

Carpenter, Ted G., <u>NATO at 40: Confronting a Changing World</u>. Lexington, MA: Lexington Books, 1990.

Cartwright, John et. al. <u>The State of the Alliance 1986-1987</u>. Boulder and London: Westview Press, 1987.

Cohen, Roger. "U.S. - French Relations Turn Icy After Cold War." <u>The New York Times International</u>, July rest of date cut off.

Coker, Christopher. Shifting into Neutral? Burden Sharing in the Western Alliance in the 1990s. London: Brassey's(UK) Ltd., 1990.

"Defence Expenditures of NATO Countries 1970-1990." Table Compiled by NATO's Statistical Analysis Service.

"Defending America: CDI Options for Military Spending." The Defense Monitor, Vol. XXI, Number 4, 1992.

"Defense of the West--America's Commitment." Center for Defense Information. June 18, 1987.

"Defense Reductions in NATO Europe." The British American Security Information Council, Jan 1992.

Drew, S. Nelson, et al. The Future of NATO: Facing an Unreliable Enemy in an Uncertain Environment. New York: Praeger Publishers, 1991.

Finnegan, Philip. "Allies' Burden-Sharing Issue Rankles Congress." Defense News, Feb 10, 1992, p. 8.

Finnegan, Philip and Hitchens, Theresa. "U.S. Cut of NATO Funds May Spur Allied Rebuff." Defense News, Oct. 12, 1992, p. 4.

Fiscarelli, Rosemary. "NATO in the 1990's: Burden Shedding Replaces Burden Sharing." Foreign Policy Briefing, CATO Institute, June 26, 1990.

Fisher, Marc. "Europeans Told of U.S. Isolationism: Congressmen Signal Slipping Commitment To Atlantic Alliance." Washington Post, Feb. 2, 1992.

Forrest, Jack. "NATO: The Essential Treaty." Imprimis, Oct 1988, p. 1-6.

Foss, Christopher F., ed., Jane's Armour and Artillery 1992-1993. Virginia: Jane's Data Division, 1992.

"Franco-German Relations in Post-Cold War Europe." The Atlantic Council of the United States, Washington, D.C., July 10, 1992.

Gaston, Charles Robert (ed.). Washington's Farewell Address, Webster's First Bunker Hill Oration, Lincoln's Gettysburg Address. Boston: Ginn and Company, 1919.

Gerlach, Jeffrey R. "Pentagon Myths and Global Realities: The 1993 Military Budget." Policy Analysis, CATO Institute, May 24, 1992.

Giltman, Maynard W. "The Justifications for Stationing American Forces in Europe 1945-1992." A paper, April 1992.

Henderson, Sir Nicholas, The Birth of NATO, Boulder, CO: Westview Press, Inc., 1983.

Hitchens, Theresa. "NATO Meeting Will Feature Peacekeeping in E. Europe." Defense News. Oct. 26, 1992.

_____. "NATO Forum To Focus On Peacekeeping Duty." Defense News. Nov 23, 1992.

Hoagland, Jim. "The Case for European Self-Defense." No source cited, no date.

House Votes to Cut Overseas Forces." The Washington Post, June 4, 1992, p. A5.

Indefensible." The Atlantic Monthly, June, 1989, p. 33.

Japan's Nuclear Buildup." Parade Magazine, Jan 10, 1993, p. 23.

Knorr, Klaus. "Burden-Sharing in NATO: Aspects of U.S. Policy." Orbis-A Journal of World Affairs, Feb 25, 1986.

Kondracke, Morton. "Who Needs NATO?" The New Republic, March 5, 1990, p. 14.

Krauss, Melvyn. "Seven Myths About NATO." Imprimis, Oct 1988, p. 1-4.

Lancaster, John. "Top General Supports 150,000 U.S. Troops in Europe as Hedge." The Washington Post, Mar. 4, 1992.

Lautenberg, Frank. "U.S. Must Spread Expense of Overseas Basing to Wealthy Allies." Remarks are excerpted from Aug. 12, 1992 speech supporting an amendment to the appropriations bill. Aug 31, 1992.

Leopold, George. "Rand Studies Defend Base Force Troop Deployment Levels." Defense News, Sept 21, 1992.

Miller, Charles. "NATO Unveils Rapid Reaction Corps." Defense News, Oct. 5, 1992.

Morrison, David C. "The Build-Down." The Atlantic Monthly, June 1989, p. 60-64.

"NATO Approves New Strategy." Arms Control Today. Nov. 1991, p. 15.

"NATO: Is It Time to Withdraw?" CATO Policy Report, no date, p. 6.

NBC. `Today Show'. Interview with General John Galvin, NATO Supreme Allied Commander. March 5, 1990.

Nelson, Daniel N. "NATO--means, but no ends." The Bulletin of the Atomic Scientists, Jan/Feb 1992, p. 10-11.

Pagonis, William G. Moving Mountains: Lessons in Leadership and Logistics from the Gulf War. Boston, MA: Harvard Business School Press, 1992.

Plesch, Daniel and Nassaurer, Otfried. NATO 2000. The British American Security Information Council Report 92.2. London: BASIC, 1991.

Plesch, Daniel T. and Shorr, David. "NATO, Down and (Soon) Out." The New York Times, July 24, 1992.

Ravenal, Earl C. "NATO: A Crisis of Will or Situation?" CATO Policy Report, Nov/Dec 1985, p. 1.

Report on Allied Contributions to the Common Defense: A Report to the United States Congress by the Secretary of Defense. May 1992.

Richter, Frank J. "Do NATO Allies Contribute Their Fair Share?" Detroit News, Mar 31, 1989, p. 18.

Scarborough, Rowan. "German wants to keep U.S. Troops in Europe." The Washington Times, March 5, 1992.

Sloan, Stanley R. "The United States and a New Europe: Strategy for the Future." CRS Report for Congress. May 14, 1990.

_____. NATO in the 1990's. New York: Pergamon-Brassey's, 1989.

Snow, Donald M., Peacekeeping, Peacemaking and Peace-Enforcement: The U.S. Role in the New International Order. Strategic Studies Institute, Feb. 1993

Stubbing, Richard A. and Mendel, Richard A. "How to Save $50 Billion A Year." The Atlantic Monthly, June 1989, p. 53-58.

Suit, William. "The Logistics of Air Power Projection." Air Power History, Fall 1991, p. x.

Summers, Harry G. Jr. "A Bankrupt Military Strategy." The Atlantic Monthly, June 1989, p. 34-40.

_____. "United States Armed Forces in Europe." The Defense of Western Europe. Dover, MASS: Auburn House Publishing Company.

Taft, William H. "One on One." Defense News. July 13-19, 1992.

"The U.S. as the World's Policeman? Ten Reasons to Find a Different Role." The

Defense Monitor. Vol. XX, Number 1, 1991.

"The Global Network of United States Military Bases." The Defense Monitor, Vol. XVIII, Number 2, 1989.

Thompson, John. "NATO Program Proves Vital." Defense News. December 7-13, 1992, p. 28.

Tyler, Patrick E. "U.S. Army Gets Flexibility on Europe Troop Levels." The New York Times International, June 18, 1992, p. A15.

U.S. and NATO: Press Background." Center for Defense Information Press Release, Feb 24, 1988.

U.S. Congress. House. Committee on Armed Services. American Military Presence Abroad. H.R. 2100, National Defense Authorization Act for Fiscal Years 1992 and 1993.

U.S. Congress. House. Committee on the Budget. 102nd Cong., Feb 5, 1992.

"Views of Private Organizations and Groups on the Atlantic Pact." Special Report on American Opinion, Department of State, April 27, 1949.

Vogel, Steve. "Germans Seek Limits On Western Forces: U.S. Resists Some New Rules on Exercises." The Washington Post, July 4, 1992.

"War Games for NATO." The New York Times, Sept. 28, 1992.

Watts, Anthony J., ed., Jane's Underwater Warfare Systems 1992-1993. Virginia: Jane's Data Division, 1992.

Weinschenk, Andrew. "Galvin Calls for NATO Preeminence." Defense Week, June 8, 1992.

"What are the Nation's Vital National Security Interests?" The Defense Monitor. May 31, 1990.

"World at War - 1992: Fewer Wars - No Danger to United States." The Defense Monitor, Vol. XXI, Number 6, 1992.

Worner, Manfred. "NATO's Major Political Tasks: Europe Needs America." Vital Speeches of the Day, Aug 15, 1991, p. 642.